MEGA

O
L~~IF~~E STORY OF A DEATH
V

ANKUR SAXENA

Inkfeathers Publishing
www.inkfeathers.com

MEGA Life Story of A Death
by Ankur Saxena
Paperback Edition

First Published in 2023 in India by

Inkfeathers Publishing
Vivek Vihar, New Delhi 110095
www.inkfeathers.com

Reading Community Partners

ISBN 978-93-90882-87-8

बोला था ना...

मरने नहीं दूंगा !

#iwontletyoudie

Disclaimer

All characters in this story are real.
Any similarity to actual events or persons, living or dead, is purely intentional and deliberate. Every single letter in this book is true to its truest sense.

They are asking me to move on.

Fools do not know how far I have come with you!

Billions of light years away from this earth…

Somewhere in the lands of the Gods…

Overheard was a conversation.

Brahma: *I have already written death for three of them.*

Vishnu: *But they appear to be good souls. Won't death be an undeserved punishment?*

Indra: *Brahma, the creator, must have written it with a purpose. Who can defy his orders?*

Narad: *But they are at Mahakaal's place. Death can't even touch them till Lord Shiva…*

Brahma: Tell Shiva, I have written what I had to; I just need **three lives…**

…to be continued

दुःख इस बात का है कि तुम मर गईं...

पर समस्या इस बात से है कि तुम तिल-तिल कर के मरीं ||

PART II OF III

PROLOGUE

"Oh, so she died in a hospital?" asked you.

"Yes, she did." I replied.

"Today's hospitals are well equipped, and the doctors are also well qualified. Must have been an easy death."

I felt like hitting on your face and continue doing so till the time you reach a well-equipped hospital with a well-qualified doctor.

And probably, you understood this by seeing my red face and tried to manage the scene…

"I mean, she was on ventilator under heavy dosage of sedatives; she won't have felt that much pain."

"Have you died earlier?"

And you went numb with this question from my side.

"Have you ever been on ventilator support?"

I continued.

"And before I punch you on your nose hard enough that you need ventilator support, just shut up."

And it wasn't just one of you; I have had multiple episodes of such sort where most of you tried justifying either your survival post Covid infection or attempted justifying her death.

I was never interested in telling you what happened to us during those tormenting thirty days of hospitalisation. For me, Megha was and is my prized possession; she was the reason for me being happy and cheerful, and her demise is the reason for having lost that cheerfulness in totality. But I never wanted to share anything with anyone—neither my previous state of happiness nor my present state of despair. They say sharing eases the pain, but it is like I do not want the pain to ease. If my happiness was mine, let the pain be mine, I will live with it, and I will die with it. Why do you guys keep poking in?

"You know, I used to do a lot of Pranayama even before Covid; that saved me." so, do you mean Megha died because perhaps she didn't do Pranayama? Are you serious? Do you really know her?

I looked at your physique with obesity sneaking out from your underarms and your love handles, and I could only smile at your ignorance.

"I started taking kadha (decoction) as soon as I got Covid."

"I will just meditate and relax, and it worked."

"My doctor was my saviour."

"I did not go outside at all."

And you guys had countless reasons to justify your survival. It was as if you did not want to talk Megha but wanted to talk yourself out. You needed a pair of ears to make yourself heard out, and luckily for you, I was made dumb by destiny!

Without you even knowing her, it appeared to me a deliberate attempt on your part to showcase that Megha might have faltered upon one or the other thing that you might have taken up during your fight against Covid, and that saved your life and took her. I mean, I could sense an element of self-indulgent apathy in your sympathy without realising that your survival was and is just a probability in play.

And then things did not stop here...

I was surprised by the kind of messages I started receiving in consolation after her demise.

"Take care, bro. I also got separated from my wife recently."

"My process of divorce is underway."

"I didn't tell you earlier; it's been three years since we got separated."

And I could not understand if you were trying to console me or trying to get some consolation from me or from my state of deprival, portraying as if your pain somehow equated to that of mine!

Has human conscience been completely laid to rest in the grave while blindfolding the basic rationale of justifying relationships?

#icantbreathe

No, it's not about the "Black Lives Matter" movement if you thought so...

But if you have been in her social circle, you perfectly know what it is all about.

For this, "I can't breathe" never bothered about the colour of your skin; it was all about a pair of spongy, air-filled, thin membraned organs located on either side of your chest which they call the **Lungs**...

Official data suggests that as on 25th April 2023, out of a total 4,48,42,447 number of Indians affected by Covid, 99% of patients recovered and were discharged from the hospital, while just 1% died. It was just a matter of chance that you (Megha) and I were put into separate bins:

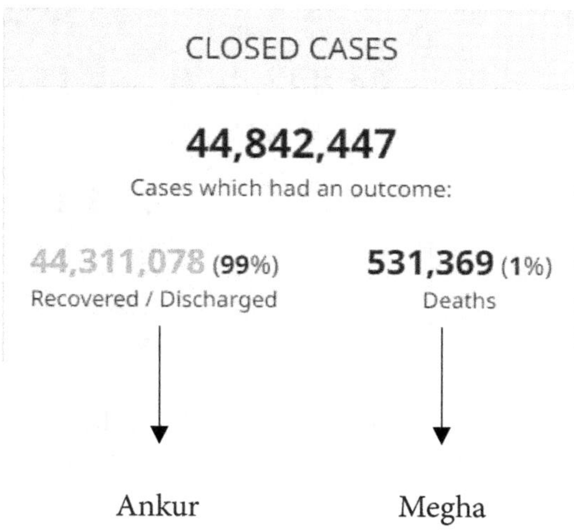

Despite such a deadly experience, humans do not appear to have learnt any lesson, for they are again back to their usual course of life—

eat, drink, and be merry without realising the fact that all of us have only a finite amount of time on this planet and be it sooner or later, we all will die for death is the ultimate truth which is least talked about.

Infact, many of you attempted to drop a discussion on her solely because she isn't alive anymore. Had it not been the case, you would have been eagerly looking out for her, as she was the lifeline of every party, every family function, every event, every outing, always smiling, ready to travel anywhere, anytime. She knew how to live every moment. Maybe she didn't have the future; she always had been the present.

If I had to redraw this correlation between Covid infection and mortality on the back of human conscience, I would redraw it in this fashion:

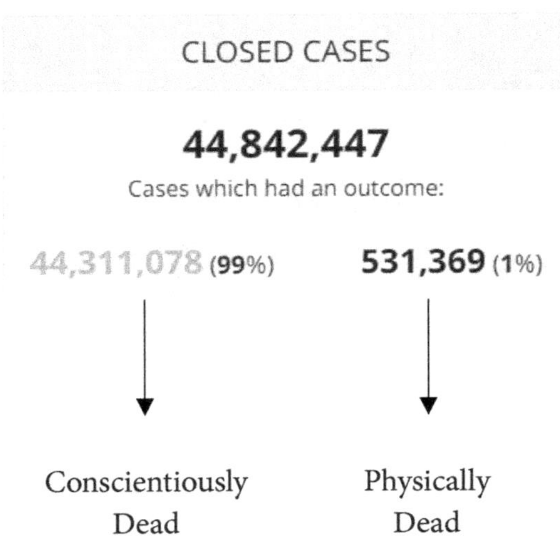

Because 99% of the humans are already dead, conscientiously dead! 99% of people have a similar routine. Getting up, having breakfast, running to their office, coming back, having dinner, sleeping, and start rubbing their.... again the next morning!

99% of humans do the same thing repeatedly without conscience or diving into the deeper aspect of human reality.

Our childhood fantasies utterly differ from our adulthood realisations, for as we grow from childhood to adolescence and then to adulthood, our dreams keep shrinking. A child who wanted to be an astronaut ends up as a school teacher, a girl who wanted to be a fashion designer ends up as a housewife. We have a huge number of compromised dreams but just one lifetime.

Life has become a Temple Run sort of game where each one of us keeps collecting coins without even having time to count or spend them, unknowingly progressing into the Blue Whale Game, ultimately meeting the ultimate truth of life—the Death—and hence 99% of humans are already dead.

But that wasn't the case with Megha!

Bringing her back to the core of our discussion, I must admit that though she lived for only 34 years, she lived a complete life.

No doubt, there remain many aspirations unfulfilled and many dreams unrealised. Yet, Megha lived each moment of her life, even those spent inside the hospital. And it is this presence of her in every moment of life that teaches us the essence of life, which has been attempted to be summed up in the book impressing upon the fact that howsoever small your identity may be, you can still leave an indelible remark on whosoever you come in contact with.

While writing this, I am reminded of the book titled, "Who will cry, when you die" by Robin Sharma.

For such an ardent soul that brought smiles to every face she met, a bubbly girl that lit up the mood, a persona that personifies life, let us all try to continue smiling without shedding even a single drop of tear from the eyes.

Covid brought us first-hand experience of how things medically progress, how things worsen, and later, how things slip off your hands in a flash. For the life, which we all are hanging up on, which seems to us a matter of a lifetime, long enough to appear having any end, it is just a thin probability.

As things medically progressed for us, we had to take medical decisions in degrading circumstances. As they say, there is always a first time for everything; we kept on googling things on our own, looking for the slightest ray of hope. The only people who could answer our concerns were those who had had such a deadly experience but such people who had had such a deadly experience were already dead!

The worst thing that happens during such a medical recourse is that one, who is so emotionally bonded to the one on the death bed, has to take very hard decisions on his/her behalf, never knowing what would be the fate of such decisions. For most of you, this would be totally unrelated and unfelt for, as it matters mostly for those for whom her life mattered. Also, Covid has given us such a deadly experience that death has become a routine word and doesn't bother us anymore. Still, death is the ultimate truth, and it has to come to each one of us.

It was me who, during her last few minutes, promised to her, ***"I won't let you die!"*** and now there remains a promise broken on my part, which despite knowing the fact that it can't be fulfilled anymore, I still can't let her slip off my hands, for a persona that carried such huge magnitudes of liveliness can't rest among the dead. This is thus a small effort on my part to make her a part of the lives of those who have the courage to read this so that she remains with all of us ***forever***.

But I have a small suggestion for those who think she died an easy death. As you start reading this book here onwards, hold your nose so that not even a single molecule of oxygen reaches your lungs. Hold it till you finish reading this book, which recounts her journey of full 30 days for which she was not able to breathe.

Breathing is a simple process of inhaling oxygen and exhaling carbon dioxide that happens reflexively on its own every second in our body, consciously or unconsciously. The only thing you have to do for now is to consciously hold it for just twenty-five lakhs ninety-two thousand seconds, the time she took to breathe her last.

Don't worry, friend, I guarantee, you won't die!

But just a small word of caution for the faint-hearted ones...

Read further at your own risk!

Low SpO2 levels ahead...

Date: 09th May 2021

Place: Balaji Skyz, Nipania, Indore

SpO2: 99

"Six!"

She screamed as she hit the sponge ball hard with the bat while three of us—me, she, and Aarohi *(our 1-year-old daughter)*—were playing cricket in the balcony of our flat on the 1st floor of Balaji Skyz, Nipania, Indore. It was her signature style to conclude the game as it got dark in the evening. I gazed at the ball that flew over my head, and left for the ground floor to bring the ball back.

We had been apart since Nov 2019. After Aarohi came to us in Sep 2019, we went to Meerut—our native place on Diwali of 2019, from Bangalore, where both of us worked, whereafter I came back to Bangalore in Nov 2019, leaving Megha and Aarohi at Aarohi's Nani's place so that Megha could enjoy her maternity leave period with her mom.

After that, the first wave of Covid struck in March 2020, and state-wise movement restrictions did not allow me to meet Megha and our newly born daughter, Aarohi, for almost a year. It was only in Sep 2020, exactly when Aarohi turned one, that I could fly to Meerut and bring them to Indore, my new place of posting.

"The child will be mine after six years of age," I said.

"Until then?" Megha asked smilingly.

"It will be the mother's prerogative."

She laughed out loud as we had this funny conversation during the days of her pregnancy.

Laughter was her signature, for if you have ever noticed her while laughing, she would keep her right hand in front of her mouth and raise her left hand pointing towards you and will laugh out loud. One could easily notice that she would always laugh from her heart. It was as if each cell, each atom, each molecule in her body was laughing. It was never a pretentious laughter. Instead, it was an infectious laughter with infection rate much higher than that of Covid.

"I don't need the water bottle," I said while leaving for the office.

"You are not taking lunch also with you nowadays to the office. Are you eating out?"

"No."

"Then why not even the water bottle?"

"Because I will have to take my mask off to drink water."

"You mean you will remain thirsty for 7-8 hours?"

"Don't you keep fast for me on Karva Chauth?" I winked at Megha smilingly and patted her cheek.

"Oh… revenge!" she smiled and gave the water bottle to me once again.

"Take this and wait; I am bringing the lunch box also."

"Megha, I won't."

And this was how I used to leave for the office during Covid days, with double mask on, and hands covered in gloves. We had further made arrangements in the office as per the Covid protocol with transparent sheets affixed across the counters to avoid any direct interaction with any visiting customer and sanitizers kept at the entrance. Anybody entering the office premises will be thermal screened to ensure no infected person visits the branch. Throughout the day, I would ensure I never remove my mask and would avoid touching my face or any other body part with gloves. Once at home, I would safely dispose off the mask and the gloves before entering. Megha would thoroughly sanitize my hands from a safe distance with her mask on. I would enter straight into one of the three bathrooms which solely I was using and take a hot water bath, even in the summers, to get rid of any of the slightest imprints of the virus that might have got stuck on somehow.

As I came up after picking the ball from the ground floor, I felt as if I was losing my breath and went directly to the kitchen to have a glass of water while she and Aarohi continued to play in the balcony.

While gulping water, I felt as if a heat wave struck me and it appeared to me that I should check my body temperature.

The thermometer beeped, and it showed

102 degrees fahrenheit.

I looked at her and Aarohi still playing in the balcony...

Despite stringent precautions, I had brought the virus home.

Date: 10th May 2021

Place: Balaji Skyz, Nipania, Indore

Time: 08:00 am

SpO2: 99

"Ankur, I have placed your tea outside your room. You can take it." she screamed.

Having confined myself to one bedroom, she called me from outside. As a matter of practice and precaution, Megha and Aarohi would go to another bedroom diagonally opposite mine before I opened my room's door and grabbed whatever was placed on the floor as soon as possible, only to shut the door back.

The last day, when I went to get tested for Covid after I developed 102-degree fever, I trembled thinking of going back home.

Should I stay in a separate room in a hotel?

Should I take a separate flat for the time being?

I had already spent the whole day in the car thinking about whether to return home. It was late evening when she called me to ask when would I return.

"Megha, I am worried about you and Aarohi."

"Don't worry; I have sanitised the whole place. I will keep the main

door open, come in and go directly into your room and stay there. I will wear a mask and re-sanitise everything. Just make sure you don't touch anything while coming in."

"But what if....?"

"If that's the case, both Aarohi and I must already be Covid positive by now; the symptoms will appear in a day or two."

That was her way of lightening whatever burden you have in your mind. She was known to make things simple and easy so that nothing appeared difficult.

Anyways, upon her insistence, I returned home at 10 in the night and went straight into my room. It was now 8'o clock the next morning, and she had kept the tea outside my room. But as I prefer letting the tea cool off before taking the first sip, let us talk tea till that time.

It was sometime in March 2014; we had got married the last month and were staying at Kalyan Nagar in Bangalore when one of her close friends came to our home for a short stay with us. Megha was preparing breakfast in the kitchen when I came out after taking a shower.

As I dressed up and reached the kitchen, I noticed how both the ladies were chit-chatting, thus making the *pakodis* spicier. I wasn't used to drinking tea till that time, a boiling hot glass of milk being my preferred choice, and Megha knew the absolute temperature I wanted the milk to be.

During breakfast, a discussion broke out of nowhere as to what makes a girl happy. Her friend had a full list of things a girl expects from her husband. Megha and I were laughing out loud at her as the list continued growing when her friend suddenly turned serious.

"But do you know what makes Megha happy?" she asked me.

I glanced at her and then at Megha. Megha was equally anxious to know what her friend had for her.

"Just a cup of tea in the morning." and both of them laughed out loud.

Megha looked at me as if nodding in affirmation. I was a master at reading her heart!

From that day till yesterday, it was me who was preparing tea every morning. Sipping this odd-tasting, brownish fluid every morning with two Parle-G biscuits had become our daily routine. As I would start reading the newspaper while having tea, she would place a video call to her sister and her parents, making sure everyone had their tea together.

To all the bachelors, to-be-married, already married guys reading this book, I have a sincere piece of advice. Preparing just a single cup of tea for your wife every morning does many wonders and is strongly recommended.

Anyhow, from a teetotaller, I had become a tea-total-her.

Meanwhile, let us return to the tea getting cold outside the room.

Wearing a mask after washing my hands, I opened the door to find a cup of tea along with 4-5 Parle-G biscuits and a piece of rusk kept on a plate on the floor. I looked for Megha and Aarohi and found them peeping from behind the almost closed door of another bedroom. As I picked up the plate and stood up, I winked at Megha as she sent me a flying kiss, and I closed the door smilingly.

The tea didn't taste well. It was as if it was tasteless. I took a second sip just to double-check if my taste buds were working, but the same thing happened twice. And then I realised that loss of taste and smell was a symptom of Covid.

I reached out to my cell phone to call Megha and tell her I had lost my sense of taste when I saw her WhatsApp message.

"Kaisi lagi sugar-free chai?"

Date: 11th May 2021

Place: Balaji Skyz, Nipania, Indore

Time: 08:00 am

SpO2: 99

I am reminded of a small story that we read in probably class VII or VIII, or I don't remember which class it was.

The title was – ***"The Bet"***

If you have read this story in your school, you know the story was about a banker and a young man who bet with each other on whether death penalty is better or worse than life in prison. The terms of the wager stated that if the young man could live in solitary confinement for 15 years, he would be given 2 million rubles.

The young man spends his time in confinement reading books. In the meantime, the banker's fortune declines, and he realizes that he will be unable to pay off the bet. The banker resolves that exactly on the day the 15 years period was going to get over, he would kill the young man so as not to owe him the money.

However, as the banker, intending to kill the young man, enters the cell where the young man had been staying, the banker finds that the young man is not there but finds a note written by him.

The note declared that during his period of confinement in the cell for the past 15 years, the young man had learned to despise material goods for the fleeting things they were.

Therefore, to demonstrate his contempt, he intends to leave confinement just five minutes before the bet is up, thus losing the bet.

Rx

- Pantocid
- Ivermectin
- Azithromycin
- Fabiflu
- Mucinac AB
- Methylprednisolone
- Montair LC
- Paracetamol
- Vit C Candies
- Syp Grillinctus
- Warm Water Gargles
- Steam

It was all okay till the set of medicines in the prescription, but as I started gargling, two more sounds started coming from outside my room...

Megha will start imitating me as I gargled, and Aarohi will start laughing out loud.

Despite being confined within your room, Megha won't let you feel alone. Finding a reason to cheer up and stay cheerful was a skill she was master at.

Further, she was so serious about Aarohi that things changed beautifully after her advent into our family. With Covid leading to Work from Home and a No Maid regime, Megha had started managing all things on her own while I was still required to go to the office on daily basis, being in the essential services sector.

After the birth of Aarohi, a normal bread-and-butter breakfast had turned into a full-fledged buffet every morning. She had put me on a high protein, fibre-rich diet that included fruit salad, dates, nuts, and yoghurt, with a pinch of traditional Indian delicacies like *poha, uttapam, idli, vada,* etc.

One night, as Aarohi slept, Megha cuddled with me and brought her mobile phone, which was unusual on her part as she followed a strict "no cell phone" rule for an hour before sleeping.

"*What?*" I asked.

"You know, the first two years of a child are the most important years of his/her life." she said while unlocking her phone.

"Is it so?" I smiled teasingly.

She pushed me away with her elbow, upset with my smiling reaction.

"You are not serious about Aarohi."

"Okay, tell me, what is it?"

"Look at this. This guy claims to have a prodigy framework that helps develop a child's full potential but says that only the first two years matter."

"So why are you worried?"

"Aarohi is already one year old."

"We still have one more year to make her a prodigy child."

I once again committed the same mistake of smiling as I said so.

She got up from the bed, locked her phone, kept it away, and returned, thumping her feet on the floor.

"Once Aarohi turns two, this same guy will come claiming that the first 3 years of the child are important and then four and then five and so on..."

She looked at me angrily while coming on to the bed again...

"This is all targeted marketing..."

Nothing helped.

"I know what they will send once we join the program; I will bring the things separately from the market. The more important thing is how much time as a parent we give to our child."

And as if I had put my hand into a beehive with my last statement.

"How much time do you give to your child Mr Saxena? A government job for namesake working from 9 am to 9 pm, Saturday, Sunday everyday working? Tell me, how much time?"

She looked so cute while complaining that I always felt I had two kids at home, both girls!

And then she made her punchline,

"Can't you spend just six thousand rupees for your daughter?" she covered herself and Aarohi with the comforter, turned her face away from me, and slept.

We never bought a separate kid's cot for Aarohi. Megha always wanted to have both Aarohi and me around. It was Megha who slept in the middle of our king-size bed. While a series of pillows by the bedside prevented Aarohi from falling, it was me doing the job of pillows for Megha while sleeping.

"Can't you spend just six thousand rupees for your daughter?" the punchline kept punching...

A few minutes later, I got up from the bed to break her "no cell phone" rule, downloaded their app, logged in with her phone number, and placed the order.

The next morning while having tea together, all three of us laughed out loud at last night's incident. She was happy for the order was already placed.

But suddenly, she got serious.

"While coming back from the office this evening, bring a drawing book and a set of water colours."

"Water colours?" I exclaimed.

She looked at Aarohi and then at me. Aarohi was busy colouring the newspaper with her set of wax crayons.

"But she is just one."

"Do as I say; she is a prodigy child now."

My stomach ached while laughing.

Fast forward to April 2023, the first six years of the child have become important.

Dear Megha

Hope you're enjoying the
Challenge with your baby!
If you want more boosters, more
advanced activities and exercises for

everything about our advanced level
program and also make you a special
offer! This program comes with a ton
of boosters, lots of new exercises, new
learning tracks, and several bonuses and
goodies for your little one! Suitable even
if your baby is older than 2 years!

Details of the session:

stable connections)

Please check your email for more details!

Thanks,

17:04

August 18, 2021

Megha died of Covid on 16th June 2021...

I am raising the Superstar now...

Regards
Aarohi's Dad

22:22

Date: 12th May 2021

Place: Balaji Skyz, Nipania, Indore

Time: 07:00 am

SpO2: 99

"Ankur, you can come out of your room now."

It was around 7 in the morning when I heard her saying this from outside my room, where I had confined myself.

"What happened?" I asked, confused, as my quarantine period wasn't over yet.

"Both me and Aarohi have 102 degrees fahrenheit on the thermometer." she replied. It was exactly what I did not want to happen.

"I will order the drinks." He said excitedly.

Her brother, his wife, and their two years old son had come from Pune to our place in Indore in March 2021 for a short trip. It had been a wonderful experience all throughout, with all of us travelling and enjoying Holi festivities together at home. Megha was so fond of travelling and exploring new places together that she won't miss out on any such opportunity. In our first 36 months after marriage, we had travelled to 36 different cities using all modes of transport, leaving no more than a few hundred bucks in my bank account but having billions of memorable incidents of enjoying ourselves together.

When I stated at the beginning of the book that Megha lived each and every moment of her life, she actually did. A restless soul with an electrifying presence and a never dying zeal to roam around had led me to many such last-minute, unplanned trips that today form the most cherished moments of my life.

With her brother and their small family, we had travelled to many places, including Ujjain—the city of *Mahakaal*, *Omkarehswar*, and *Maheshwar*, during their short stay with us.

"Megha, I will order LIIT for you. Give it a try; you will like it." her brother said.

The rooftop cafe in Indore had a wonderful ambience with an equally wonderful menu. The only thing we didn't know was that the odds were soon going to turn against us. As I stated earlier, life is a thin probability, we had started walking on the edge by now.

The first wave of Covid was over, and travel movement restrictions were now lifted. Every dauntless soul that wanted to inhale fresh oxygen craved to come out, travel and explore. We were no exception, totally unaware that a soothing breeze of oxygen would soon lay the foundation for oxygen support.

Megha developed skin allergy after having LIIT, and red marks appeared all over her face and entire body the very next day. Though there was no irritation and no itching, we went from doctor to doctor, including skin specialists in Indore, but the marks just won't go away.

All doctors had the same underlying salt combination on their prescriptions—Levocetirizine and Methylprednisolone—only the names of the medicines changed. But nothing changed for Megha. The marks just won't fade out.

When things didn't improve for almost a month, I got her blood test done on 29th April 2021, which no doctor had prescribed till now. The test revealed that her CRP was inflated and beyond the desirable range.

No, it was not Covid yet, for the game of death had just begun...

The virus was soon going to get a body fertile enough to make a killing.

Megha tested Covid positive on 12th May 2021.

Patient Name	: MRS. MEGHA TYAGI	Reg. Date	: 12/05/2021 16:00:41
Age & Sex	: Year/Female	Accession Date	: 12/05/2021 16:00:41
Reg. No.	:	Authorize Date	: 12/05/2021 16:00:54
Perm. No.	:	Report Date	: 12/05/2021 16:01:02
Referred by	: SELF	Center Name	:
Sample Type	: Swab	Vial ID	:

Parameter	Results	Units	Reference Range
Covid 19 Rapid Antigen test			
Covid 19 Rapid Antigen test	: POSITIVE	-	NEGATIVE

NOTE : COVID 19 rapid antigen test is for information only. The confirmatory test for COVID 19 is RT-PCR.

Test Method : Rapid card

---End Of Report---

Date: 13th May 2021

Place: Balaji Skyz, Nipania, Indore

SpO2: 99

Life had become a little easier. The doctor confirmed we did not need separate confinement anymore. So, we took medicines together, took steam together, and yes, not to forget, gargled together. Aarohi would stare at both of us, gargling, and as usual, laughter will break out.

Aarohi was also positive and developed coughing. She did not have any fever and was advised medicines for mouth ulcers. Covid had different symptoms for different age groups.

So far, vaccination was not available for people below 45 years of age. Megha had incessantly tried to get registered for Covid vaccination. Despite being classified under essential services requiring my continuous presence at the office, vaccination was not administered to me being below the prescribed age group. By the time, slots opened for under 45 people, we had already caught up the infection.

"Remember the rat?" she asked while we were having dinner that night.

Just a few weeks ago, Megha was doing her office work on her laptop in the living room, which had a huge, around 450 square feet in size, balcony attached to it. This was the same balcony where we used to play cricket in the evening with the sponge ball. Since the flat was on the 1st floor, it would happen that, at times, pigeons or rats would come onto the balcony, which had a sliding glass door for entry and exit.

I was resting near Aarohi in the bedroom, waiting for Megha to come in, when I heard her screaming...

"Ankur, Ankur, Ankur..."

I ran towards the living room where she was and followed her eyes.

A rat entered the living room from a small gap between the wall and the door, which probably I hadn't shut properly. The rat climbed vertically up the curtains and then horizontally over the curtain rod, attempting to come down from the other side.

While coming down, the rat fell on to the wall-mounted open showcase and then fell directly on the floor with a photo-printed mug falling directly on its head, and Megha screamed.

The rat stayed there for around a second and then ran away towards the balcony through the same gap from where it had entered.

Megha looked at the broken mug, which had a few stains of blood, as I opened the balcony door to double-check.

There laid the rat, still, in the middle of the balcony—**Dead!**

Both of us looked at each other for a second. It was as if everything happened in a flash. I shut the balcony door properly this time and sat with Megha in the living room.

"This rat came only to die?"

Megha was such a sensitive girl that even plucking a flower would traumatise her. I remember while going to Hampi on a trip, driving our car; she saw a lot of trees being felled for construction of the highway, and tears started rolling down her eyes as she cursed humans for such wrong doings.

I fully understand that this incident was such a small one that it could better have been omitted from the book. Still, she had brought the rat to the core of our discussion on 12th May 2021.

"Remember the rat?"

Date: 14th May 2021

Place: Balaji Skyz, Nipania, Indore

SpO2: 99

"Come on, guys. Everybody out of bed. Fast, it's Yoga Time."

It was early in the morning. I was still sleeping in my separate room while Megha and Aarohi slept in another bedroom. I am an early riser and always wake up early to catch hold of a book and read for at least an hour. But Yoga was not my cup of tea.

But for Megha, Yoga was the first thing that should mark the beginning of the day. You liked it, or you didn't, Yoga was supposed to be done first thing in the morning. She would drag me onto the Yoga mat and become my Yoga trainer. Her perfect manoeuvres and yogic postures were charismatic. I would fall in instant love.

"*10 times.*" I looked at her as if ten was a big number.

Megha had asked me to do Surya Namaskaras at least ten times every morning.

The count later kept increasing with my weight increasing faster than the count.

"*You don't do it by heart.*" she complained one day.

"I do it for you." I submitted.

"That is why it is not working on you, do it for yourself." She sounded a little worried about my health.

Health was her number one priority, and she will give her hundred percent to it and it was because of this she always wanted you to give your hundred percent to your health.

While I was the one who would always find an excuse to order food on Zomato and Swiggy, she was totally opposite to me in this context. She was not a great cook, but she always had a simple menu in mind for dinner. Ordering food from outside was almost prohibited at home unless it was she who wanted to relish upon it, that too rarely.

"Aarohi ke Papa, look who is there on the Yoga mat?"

And I saw Aarohi sitting in front of Megha, both facing each other on either corner of the Yoga mat doing *kapalbharati.*

It was a sight to behold. Aarohi was copying Megha perfectly. Her stomach would go in immediately after Megha's, and they would laugh out while exhaling.

I sat on the floor for around 10-15 minutes doing the same with them and then got up, giving the excuse of preparing the tea.

Date: 15th May 2021

Place: Balaji Skyz, Nipania, Indore

SpO2: 99

"Send me a pic on daily basis." She said on the video call, and I nodded in affirmation.

Megha was a fitness freak, while I was an introvert bookworm. The time Megha would spend doing Yoga and exercise, I would prefer investing the same time in reading a book. But with the slightest increase in my blood cholesterol levels, Megha had taken upon herself the task of bringing it back to normalcy. While we were in Bangalore, our conflicting interests made us reach an agreement as per which I would get up early as usual, read whatever I wanted to, and then prepare tea for both of us as she got up around an hour later, but...

....I would have to come an hour earlier from the office and join her for a one-hour Power Yoga Class in the evening near our residence in Koramangala.

Now many of you nowadays have such things called as couple goals, but all such stuff came naturally to us without indulging in any public show-off. I cared for her, and she cared for me, and hence nothing required serious deliberations at any point of time. It was like we were always together with each other. While I always hated moving my waist round and round and practising any yoga move, I loved seeing her doing the same with such perfection that she appeared a Yoga Trainer to me. Each of her Yoga moves had two elements—one, of great seriousness towards how a particular posture engages with and heals up your body, and two, a hidden element of amour as she knew I was constantly gazing at her during the entire session.

It was like whenever we breathed in and breathed out, romance was in the air!

Every night post-dinner, two of us would go for a walk and discuss the whole day's happenings with each other. People say one should not talk office at home, but it was totally the opposite in our case. I would discuss my office issues with her, and she would discuss her with mine. We both were counsellors for each other. Her insights into my office issues and my delving into her office issues would improve the situation for both of us.

We have come to an era where every human possesses a pair of lips to speak, but none wants to use the ears. Everybody has opinions, but none wants to listen to the other. But here, the two of us were complimentary to each other. Office tension was never a cause of worry when she was around. The ears used to listen while the lips were meant to get locked.

Date: 16th May 2021

Place: Balaji Skyz, Nipania, Indore

SpO2: 99

How can a tiny, microscopic object like a Covid virus weigh so heavily upon a well-built, athletic physique with a powerful set of lungs that routinely do all sorts of yoga kriyas?

Had there been a choice, I would have been a better candidate for fatality as I avoided exercising, had a sedentary lifestyle, and exercised no restraint on eating habits while she was super-fit badminton and tennis player with an active lifestyle and a controlled healthy diet.

When she asked me to send a pic on daily basis, she wanted to keep a check on whether I was following the daily exercise routine in her absence. At this time, Megha and Aarohi were at her parents' place in Meerut while I had returned to Bangalore in Nov 2019.

It was pre-covid era, and people could move anywhere, anytime, without restrictions. Since she was away from me, she subscribed for a 6 months Cultfit pack in my name, a period that tallied exactly with her maternity leave period, to ensure that I kept following the routine. I would go to Cultfit on daily basis and send her a selfie, thus marking my so-called biometric attendance. This was how we never missed each other. Since after delivery, she was advised not to do strenuous exercises for at least six months; she caught up my habit. Though she was also fond of reading books, she wasn't a regular reader. But during this period, she started reading books daily; and every evening, we started having discussions on whatever we read that day.

Like this, my book reading speed had got doubled. Not only this, but we were also finishing two books together.

Strength lies in differences and not in similarities.

Stealthily before marriage, I had checked our horoscopes and told Megha that only four of the thirty-six stars were matching. We were a perfect mismatch! But ours was a love marriage, and I did not want stars to come in my way of getting united with my moon.

But if just four stars can deliver such magnitudes of happiness and togetherness, I don't think people need more stars to tally.

Infinite love does not need finite number of stars...

Date: 17th May 2021

Place: Balaji Skyz, Nipania, Indore

SpO2: 92

It was early in the morning; Aarohi had just woken up while I had just got up reading a book. As I passed through the bathroom, I saw Megha with teary eyes in the reflection of the bathroom mirror...

I hurried onto her, asking what had happened.

"I can't breathe." she replied.

Now this was exactly the fifth day which, they say, decides the progression of the infection that the virus causes. I brought her Oxymeter immediately to check if her oxygen levels were dropping.

The readings started from 87 against the usual 96-97 range and later stabilized at 92. We looked at each other while Aarohi stared at us, thinking about which game we were playing. I removed the Oxymeter from her finger and placed it on the index finger of another hand. No change. The same thing happened twice. It showed 92.

"Are we going to the hospital?" she asked.

"Yes, all three of us."

"All three? But why you and Aarohi?"

"We will stay with you only."

"Ankur, I am okay. Just think about Aarohi."

"Jaha jayenge, sath me jayenge."

As I started packing things for the hospital, Megha opened the refrigerator door and peeped inside.

"How many days may it take at the max?" she asked while staring inside the fridge.

"No idea." I responded.

"It's full of cream here. Let me make ghee out of it; else the cream will get spoilt."

I looked at her surprisingly.

"You weren't able to breathe just a few hours back."

"So am I right now! But why waste things? It won't take me more than an hour, and by that time, you will also get ready packing the bags."

Lakshmi of my house was still concerned about my grahasthi!

With an inflated set of D-Dimer, CRP, IL6, and thorough consultation with the doctor, we stood at the hospital's reception for admission. She held Aarohi in her arms as I completed the admission formalities for all three of us.

Surprisingly, she had scored 0/25 in the CT scan just a day before.

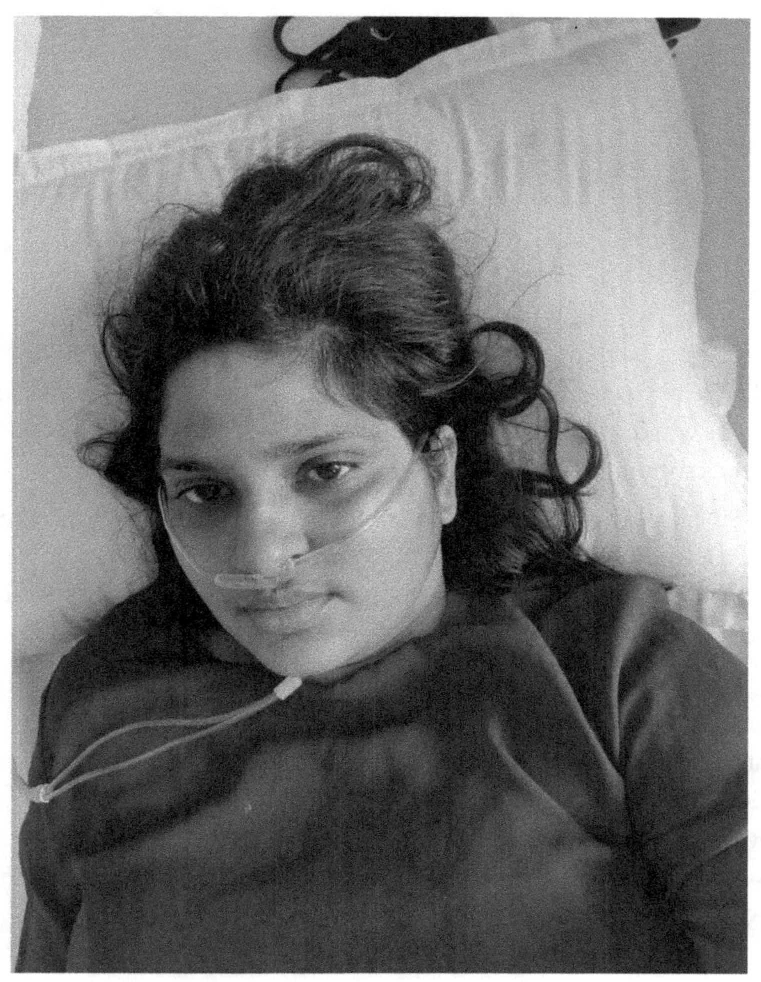

Date: 18th May 2021

Place: Hospital Room No. 505

SpO2: 94

All three of us were in the same room—me, Megha, and Aarohi. The room's window opened towards the main road, offering a scenic view of the city and the sky.

Since Megha was placed on minor oxygen support, I had taken upon the responsibility of Aarohi to ensure the mother gets complete rest and Aarohi's mischiefs do not trouble her and do not disrupt the medical set-up around Megha.

Megha had a small pipe-like tube inserted into her nose which did not cover the mouth. So as of now, she had no problem speaking or eating on her own. Everything was normal, but the nose tube was an additional apparatus affixed to the human body. Once the oxygen levels caught up, we would be all home. They had administered dosages of Remdesivir to her as per the standard Covid treatment protocol, and it was her second day on Remdesivir.

"Did you send Simha Kriya video to Sir?" she asked.

Sir is one of the finest human beings I have ever met. He was diagnosed Covid positive just a few days back and was hospitalised in Meerut due to declining SpO2 levels. He is the sole son of his family and his work in the field of education, training hundreds of civil services aspirants, working all day and night for the student community, is beyond parlance.

I had been one of his students aspiring for civil services after the recession of the year 2008 shattered our dreams post completing graduation. I had cleared the prelims and was up for Mains when I told sir,

"I am flying to Bangalore."

"Good, when will you be back?" sir asked. He is a travel enthusiast and loves exploring new places.

"I am going to Bangalore permanently. I am not coming back."

He was confused. One of his brightest students had qualified prelims and should have been seriously preparing for Mains, but here was I, in a completely another world of mine, as for this magistrate inside me, my district was there in Bangalore. Megha had started working as a Software Engineer in Bangalore after her post-graduation, and I was bound to go. The call of love resounded more than the call of duty.

Sir took me inside his newly bought car. We sat inside the car with the AC on in the burning summer of 2013. Sir was a master in the art of convincing. As he continued with his logic and pointers on how essential it was for not only me but also for him and his coaching institute that I should continue with my preparations, I opened the car door after around 2 hours of discussion. It was late at night.

Love triumphed!

"Hi, I need an oxygen cylinder here in Meerut. My brother is Covid positive and unable to breathe."

His message flashed on our common group of college mates where we used to chit-chat. He was one of my classmates in college and was residing in Meerut. There had been multiple instances where people needed hospitalization, ICU beds, oxygen cylinders, and what not during such times of crisis when Covid was at its peak. All such stuff was running short because of the high positivity rate among people, and the second wave was proving to be a killer.

"Ankur, see if you have somebody known in Bhopal. My uncle is positive, and there is no bed available. He is not able to breathe."

"Your DZM is Covid positive, and his SpO2 levels have dropped significantly. Do you know someone who can arrange a hospital bed?"

"One more oxygen cylinder, please...."

"The fellow needs an immediate blood transplant. Please check if you have any O+ person in your office."

"His wife called stating that he will not be able to come to the office; he has been hospitalized being Covid positive."

"Urgent, needed Remdesivir for immediate administration at hospital."

I responded to each and every call of anybody in distress, known or unknown, running from pillar to post, ensuring nobody suffered. We also formed a WhatsApp group to ensure that all such distress calls were answered timely and arrangements made by any of us did not get duplicated at a time when medical facilities and equipments were running scarce.

"Sir, he has been discharged from the hospital yesterday, and he wants to resume office from tomorrow." My junior asked me in case he could join after getting Covid affected.

"Hi, happy to know that you have been discharged from the hospital. Take care of yourself, stay at home for another 7-8 days; I will sanction your leave. In case you do not have sufficient leave balance, I will give you work from home, but take care. Do not worry about anything here in the office. Reach out to me in case you need any assistance."

For me, the safety of each and every person working with me was of utmost importance.

And then, there came this one just a few weeks back.

"Friends, I need one Tocilizumab for my husband. People are saying it would cost some 2.40 lakh rupees. Please help me."

We were not able to arrange Tocilizumab from anywhere. It was not available in any medical store that we enquired about. In those days, Tocilizumab had become a dreadful name on two accounts—one—the name suggested that the person was in super critical condition and an immediate and timely administration of this medicine was yet more super critical for his or her survival and two—the medicine was running heavily short all over India.

Seeing me anxious about being unable to arrange Tocilizumab for the lady, Megha came to me and checked the lady's WhatsApp message. *"Ankur, it appears the lady needs money. Check if the medicine is available at her place somehow."*

I called her and asked if she could arrange the medicine from somewhere, and we could help her with the amount. She confirmed that the medicine was available there. But she was running short of money, with her husband not in a condition to respond.

Within next 3 hours, the contribution amount was sufficient enough for her to make the purchase. The guy came back home smiling.

"Did you send simha kriya video to Sir?" she asked again.

Both of us were concerned about his health.

"I will do it right away."

"But why not till now? I sent it to you two days back. You know how important every second is in this disease. I thought you were concerned about him. Give me his number; I will send it across."

I showed her two blueticks on my WhatsApp to Sir, and it was only after this that she calmed down.

Date: 19th May 2021

Place: Hospital Room No. 505

SpO2: 97

Fortunately, at a time when there was an acute shortage of hospital beds and oxygen cylinders, we were lucky to get admission into one of the finest hospitals in Indore. Her parameters were supposed to improve in a day or two. She had been maintaining oxygen levels above 90 with normal oxygen support.

"The doctor has asked you to arrange this medicine by evening." The nurse came with a slip in her hand.

"Tocilizumab." I felt shivers running down my spine as I opened the slip.

I looked at Megha. She smiled.

"Tocilizumab?" she asked.

I was not even required to tell her. She had read the name through my eyes. She took a deep breath, and the oxygen apparatus around her made a coking sound.

"Hey hey hey... Megha look at me; we have got the best hospital, easily got the beds available, sufficient supply of oxygen, the best set of doctors, one of the finest nursing staff, even the Covid wave is now getting over."

"But you could not arrange Tocilizumab last time, you remember?"

"Are you worried about Tocilizumab?"

She preferred remaining quiet.

"You see, I will arrange it in 2-3 hours."

Megha smiled at me.

The biggest advantage of being in a direct customer-facing service sector is that you keep meeting so many persons and personalities throughout your career span that you develop a huge social circle. While I was new in Indore, one of our staff members did everything to ensure that the medicine reached us through the hospital.

"Sir, please keep this medicine safely with you; the nurses will come and administer it in a while."

I looked at the clock; it hadn't been more than 3 hours to get the medicine delivered, and then I looked at Megha.

Megha smiled at me again.

"Happy Marriage Anniversary, Mom & Dad!"

She placed a video call from her phone wishing my parents on their marriage anniversary. However bad the circumstances may be, she would never miss any opportunity to call her near and dear ones. Photos and videos were not only her hobby but also an integral part of her life. She won't miss out on capturing any such opportunity into pixels.

It would happen every alternate weekend that she would ask to go out for a cup of coffee, and there used to be two modes of travel—one, if she had asked to take the car's keys along, it would mean that we would be driving at least 30km for this coffee, and two, if she had not asked for the car's keys, we would be walking at least 5-6 km to find an altogether new coffee shop in Bangalore.

Coffee was yet another addition to our menu of drinks, as she was very fond of the typical filter coffee of South India. Once, when we visited Coorg, we stayed in a resort that was sort of a homestay with coffee plantations all around. Megha would deeply delve into whatever new she came across. She discussed the entire process of coffee manufacturing with the owner of the resort, as he stood there supervising the labour in the segregation of coffee beans. Megha had a very minute sense of observation, and nothing could go unnoticed from her. It was this interest of her in everything new that she came across that she had a thorough knowledge of almost everything on this planet.

On each of our trips to any of the places we visited, Megha would stand in front of the boards or displays where the description of the site or its historical significance is mentioned. While most of us just click a pic on the go and leave such details unread and unnoticed, she used to read every scripture to understand how and why such a monument was built. Because of this, Megha had many real-life stories to narrate whenever any discussion on such topics popped up. Her practical understanding of each and every subject matter that came up for discussion, along with substantial evidences that she would draw from history, was highly applauded in her social circle.

Just after the video call got over, the doctor came for a visit. He looked worried seeing the medical records kept by the side of her bed.

"Any improvement?" I asked.

"Tocilizumab may take some more time to show effect." He said while staring away from us. His eyes said that something was not good.

"The staff will update you in case of any other requirement." He left. It was probably 6 or 7 in the evening.

"Plasma Therapy discontinued. Is Remdesivir the next?"

The news flashed on the TV channels as we waited for our dinner to arrive in our hospital room. Megha was already on Remdesivir. Wasn't there any specific fool proof line of treatment for Covid? Were we just part of an experiment? What about Tocilizumab? Was this also an experiment on the human body, or was it really a shield against Covid? But that guy for whom we contributed for Tocilizumab got better and returned home happily. When will it work on Megha? When will her SpO2 levels improve? When will we return home?

Amidst this melee of thoughts flashing up in mind, the hospital staff came at around 7:30 pm, advising that Megha was required to be shifted to ICU. Her last few hours' readings suggested a decline in oxygen levels with increased oxygen support.

We looked at each other and then at Aarohi. Aarohi had never stayed without her at any point of time. Infact, I was new to her, having stayed away for almost a year.

"Can things be arranged here?" the mother asked the nursing staff for the sake of her daughter.

"It would probably be a 2-3 days stay in the ICU at max, after which you will be brought back to the room." replied the hospital staff.

"Will I be allowed to meet her?" I asked.

"It would be more appropriate if the doctors advise you on this."

"Okay, remove these drips and mask. I will go along."

"These can't be removed now; we cannot take any chance, do inform us whenever you feel like visiting the washroom."

She was made to lie on a bed with an oxygen cylinder under it and a mask fitted on her face as she gazed at us together.

Now, there are 4-5 scenes that come alive, and I see things happening again each night before sleep. This scene is one of them and comes alive while writing this. She was fearless, and I was equally clueless; I never wanted her to go away from me.

While Aarohi looked blank, I probably looked a little tense, and as usual, she realized this.

"Aa rahi hoon, ja nahi rahi."

I was permitted to visit her in ICU whenever I wanted.

Date: 20th May 2021

Place: ICU Bed No. 17

SpO2: 97

I was stuck.

I had one-year-old Aarohi with me and an entire floor full of Covid positive patients while Megha was in the ICU fighting against this deadly virus on her own. I had to leave Aarohi with either the nurses or other Covid positive patients and then go two floors down to see her. But then there was no other choice.

"What is Aarohi doing?"

"She is with the nurse."

"Did she cry?"

"Not at all; she is like her mom."

"Of course she is!"

With this, a smile appeared on her face, which immediately turned into seriousness.

"Ankur, arrange a notebook for Aarohi; she must be getting bored confined in a single room. Add to it a drawing book, some pencils, and wax colours. Don't show TV or mobile phone to her. Engage her in some creative stuff."

"I will. Tell me, how are you feeling now?"

"I am okay, but I do not like the atmosphere here. Look around; all patients are almost dead on the bed, nobody moving, nobody eating, nobody to talk to, almost half dead, just breathing, that too, on oxygen support."

"Focus on yourself, Megha."

"I am. Look at this."

She pulled up a respirometer from behind her pillow and showed it to me. The third ball didn't hit the top.

"I am able to move just two of them for now."

"Don't overexert Megha; the third ball will move too. It's just a matter of some more time."

"Okay, listen, make sure Aarohi gets to eat some fruits on daily basis besides the hospital food."

I smiled at her because I was reminded of something.

"Fruits or dry fruits?"

"Fruits."

"You mean Mangoes?"

It was around 5 in the evening. Indore District authorities had made it a 10 am to 2 pm affair for office goers due to the severe second wave of Covid & as such, I used to return home by 3 pm.

We were in the bedroom. I was playing with Aarohi on the bed while Megha was working from home and doing her office work on her laptop, sitting on the bean bag opposite the bed near the balcony attached to the bedroom, when my phone rang. I have a habit of attending all calls on my cell phone with the loudspeaker on so that I do not have to hold the phone in hand, and I did so as usual.

"Namaste, Sir." the voice was of an official of one of our renowned

customers.

"Namaste, Namaste, how are you?"

"All good, sir. I needed your address."

"Branch address?"

"No sir, house address. Sir has sent a basket of Alphonsos for you."

Megha looked at me with her laptop in her lap. Now while I am writing this, I can't stop laughing, for I clearly remember her face with eyes almost popping out of her spectacles that resembled the eyes of a cat—a little serious towards the ongoing office work on the laptop and a little tempted for her favourite fruit being discussed on the conversation between me and my client. It was as if she had already smelled the Alphonsos.

"Please convey my thanks to sir. However, request you to please send them to the branch address. I will distribute them among all staff members."

She stood up from the bean bag, looking at me, keeping her laptop aside.

Since I knew what was going on in her mind, I immediately disconnected the call.

"What's the problem with you?" Megha asked.

"You know my habit."

"No, tell me, what's the problem with you?"

I was lying on my stomach when she sat on my back. Aarohi was staring at us smilingly.

"I do not like such formalities Megha, particularly from customers."

"But tell me, what's your problem?"

"I will bring you Alphonsos from the market." Aarohi had joined her mom in her ride on my back.

The phone started ringing again. It was the same customer. I turned my face around and could notice the glow in her eyes. She picked the call up and handed over the phone to me, her eyes saying, *"Tell him your address."*

"Hello."

"Sir has already sent a separate basket for the branch. This one is for you, and I am presently coming myself to deliver it to you. Please share your Google location."

I looked at Megha and gave her a cunning smile.

"Send this to the branch address."

Megha literally jumped on me, seeing the Alphonsos slipping off her hands. Aarohi repeated her Mom's gestures.

"Aarohi, do you want to eat mangoes?" Megha asked, and Aarohi immediately nodded in a yes!

That was enough for a husband and a father!

"Ummm... Okay, I have sent you my location on WhatsApp."

Alphonsos were delivered at home. She could have just 2 of them as we landed in the hospital soon after.

Megha smelling the Alphonsos immediately after home delivery.

Date: 21st May 2021

Place: ICU Bed No. 17

SpO2: 94

"Can you sing a song?" Megha asked.

"I always wanted to marry a girl who could sing."

"Oh s..t! You got cheated!" she exclaimed wittingly.

"Nope... it is now that I realise you need a listener too."

And I would take out my *Yamaha PSR i455* synthesiser once a month on the weekend and play songs while singing along. She will keep listening from the kitchen and will shout out loud from the kitchen itself in case I missed any note. She wasn't a good singer but a good connoisseur of music. Sometimes, she would come out of the kitchen asking to play songs on her demand. A few minutes later, as the breakfast would be ready, she would place the breakfast on the dining table and come to me and sit on a chair opposite where I was singing while playing the instrument, listening with utmost seriousness and telling me where I went wrong while singing.

I would play my favourite songs on our home-theatre set up and sing along standing on the dewan in the drawing room while holding the remote of the music system as a mic in my hand, and she would come running, sit on the sofa in front of the dewan and start waving her hands up in the air as if in a music concert. It was only until she caught hold of the remote from me that she would play her Punjabi party songs and start dancing along. Life was such fun.

"It's been five days now. I am getting bored here. Can you sing a song?"

I looked around in the ICU. People were lying unconscious on their beds. I could understand what trauma my girl was going through all alone as I could come to see her only for 15 minutes four times a day.

"Don't worry; they won't listen."

She looked around as I did. The nurses were busy shuffling from one bed to another, keeping track of the medication given to each patient.

"Please."

I looked into her eyes and felt like lying down on the same bed, filling her up in my arms, wearing the same oxygen mask as she did, feeling the same as she felt, suffering the same pain as she did.

Fast forward to March 2023, as I am writing this book; I haven't been able to sing since then. *Yamaha PSR i455* finds some place in the store, lying untouched with dust settled all over it.

I try staying strong; the voice breaks!

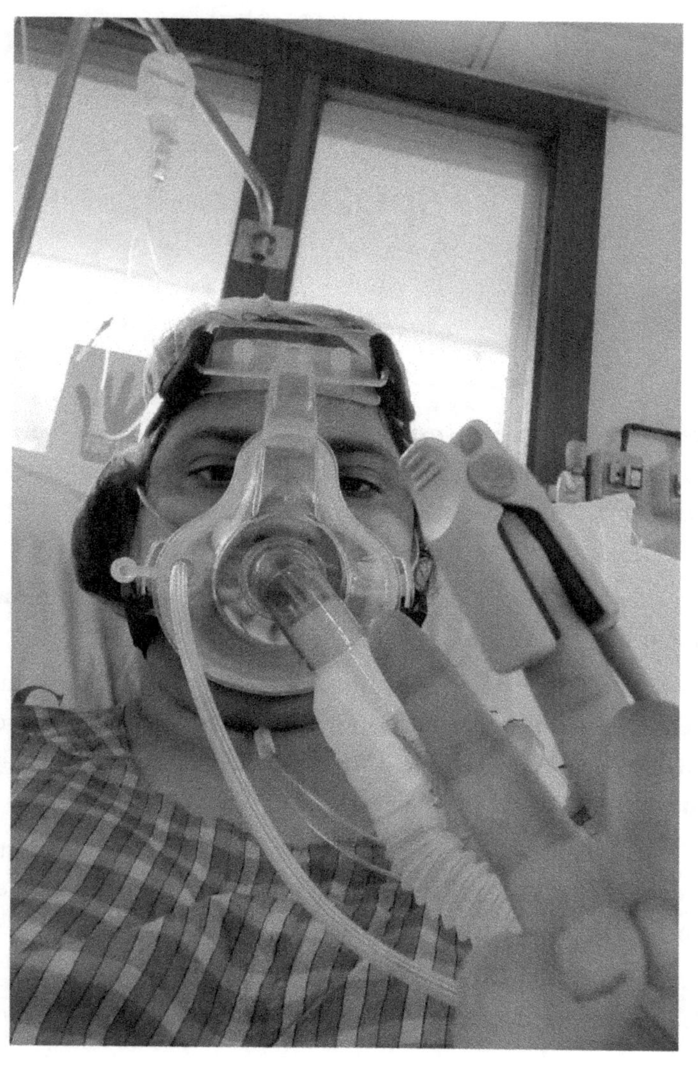

Date: 22nd May 2021

Place: ICU Bed No. 17

SpO2: 90

"Take me away from here, ask them to shift me to a normal room, and make arrangements there. I will manage everything from a normal room." Her WhatsApp message flashed on my screen at 12:18 pm. I had just come back to our room after meeting her.

I rushed back to her to check what had happened, leaving Aarohi crying in the nurse's lap.

As the lift's door opened, I saw a body wrapped in white lying on a stretcher with hospital staff waiting for the lift door to open. I hurried to Megha's bed in the ICU. She looked at me and then at the bed adjacent to her.

"They couldn't save him." That was the body of the person lying on the bed adjacent to her. I stood fixed for a second and then tried to console her. This was the first time I saw her in trauma, and she saw a live death!

"They tried for almost half an hour. Ask them to shift me to a normal room."

I went to the doctor immediately.

"We also want her to get shifted to a normal room asap. However,

her condition does not permit this. The kind of dedicated care she will get in the ICU is impossible in a normal room. Motivate her to bear for a few more days, and she will be perfectly fine."

The doctor said he would arrange a psychiatrist visit for her the next day. I was told that was usual for patients in the ICU; many had had similar experiences and benefitted from a psychiatrist's session.

I wondered how a lady known for cheering up the mood now needed a psychiatrist to cheer her up.

Date: 23rd May 2021

Place: ICU Bed No. 28

SpO2: 91

"Ask them to bring something good to eat. I am sick with the hospital food."

I had spilled over everything we bought from Star Bazaar near Forum Mall, Bangalore, in the drawing room of our Bangalore flat, but it was nowhere.

Megha was moving here and there inside the flat, cunningly trying to hide and not to let our eyes meet. As I tried looking for the bill to check whether we had bought it or had mistakenly left it there, I screamed.

"Where is Maggie?

As we went shopping for groceries together, I would keep filling the shopping cart with a variety of biscuits, namkeens, noodles, sauces, spreads, and particularly Maggie.

Megha would keep emptying the cart of any such stuff put in by me by the time we reached the billing counter. Taste was my priority; her priority was health.

Infact, one day, when I was posted in Indore, it happened that she called me over the phone when I was in the office.

"Ankur, I have finalised some items in the Big Basket app, check if you need anything else, and I will place the order."

"I am in the office, Megha."

"You stay in the office from 9 am to 9 pm, no Saturdays, no Sundays, we aren't left with even monthly ration at home. I have already added the items to the cart. Will that take more than a minute for you?"

Indore was a tough assignment in terms of official posting as the branch suffered from many chronic legacy issues, and I was finding it difficult to manage it in the absence of proper manpower. Our practice of going out together for groceries shopping was marred by the Covid wave, and also, Aarohi was just a year old to be taken outside for shopping. Time was yet another factor I was fighting for.

"Okay, I will check and confirm."

Three hours later, at around 02:30 pm, Megha called again.

"You haven't done it yet."

"Megha, I told you I am in office."

"This is your lunchtime. Get up from your seat."

It had happened at times that I returned home without even having lunch. Sometimes it used to get too hectic at the office.

"I will take lunch a little later."

"I am placing a video call. Get up for your lunch immediately and finalise the cart doing lunch."

"All right, Madam."

As usual, you had no choice but to agree with Megha, and I loved that.

I added 15-20 more items and sent her a WhatsApp confirmation.

I reached home at 09:30 pm. The Big Basket order was timely delivered and was lying all around in the drawing room. None of the items I had added were ordered!

She smelled it while changing the sofa covers in the drawing room. It was a lazy Sunday morning for us. Bangalore is a place known for its round-the-year pleasant weather, cool breeze, a charismatic fragrance, making it a perfect place for 24 by 7 romance.

"Are you making Maggie?" she landed in the kitchen to catch her ever-hungry thief.

As I prepared the 2 minutes instant noodles, she continued with her 2 minutes instant pravachanas from the drawing room, telling me how such eating habits weigh heavily on one's health, why fast food and instant noodles should be avoided, what number of calories do such items have and blah blah.

Meantime, with an equally unwavering intent of relishing the monosodium glutamate-filled delicious noodles, I served Maggie in two plates, topped them up with coriander leaves, finely cut green chillies, and just a little bit of grated paneer and placed the plates on the dining table where she was sitting reading the newspaper.

She looked at the tempting looking serving and then at me and then back at the noodles,

"Is ke sath kuchh cold coffee bhi bana lete."

And laughter broke out as usual.

Date: 24th May 2021

Place: ICU Bed No. 28

SpO2: 94

Megha probably had got accustomed to ICU happenings by now. People all around were dying one after another. Once a bed got cleared, another patient would come in. It was like a never-ending process of admission, medication, suffocation, and then permanent relaxation. Once, during my visit to the ICU, the patient's condition degraded; doctors gave their best to revive him, but a few minutes later, his family came inside crying and taking the body.

"Did you just notice how instantly a living creature gets converted into a body?"

I attempted to console her, caressing her on her forehead as that was the only area on her face that was left uncovered by medical equipments. She had an oxygen mask that tightly covered her nose with two broad strings across her cheeks towards her back, leaving greyish marks on her cheeks. They had also inserted a tube from the right side of her lower abdomen, probably for excretion, as she was not allowed to move because of drop in oxygen levels without support. Her left hand was further pierced to let the intravenous saline drip into the body. At the same time, a lot of blood samples were taken from her right hand each day to monitor her essentials.

The blood pO2 level had significantly decreased.

"Stretch, stretch, stretch, come on, no going back. Yes, Perfect."

After she was done with her yoga session, she would turn into a yoga trainer and drag me on to the yoga mat.

Twenty-five surya namaskars every morning was her daily ritual, while I always did namaskara to it from a distance.

The body, she would say, is the most artful creation of God.

It was our first trip after marriage to Manali in Feb 2014. As usual, I had gotten up earlier than Megha as she lay in my arms in our hotel room with a white quilt spread on the hotel's white bedsheet. Her face was resting on my shoulder. I kissed her forehead as she stretched lazily inside the quilt. I got up, moving towards the window on the other side of the bed facing the Himalayas.

As I drew the curtains apart, allowing the sunlight to enter the room, a scenic view of the mighty mountains caught my attention. There was snow all around, as if the entire planet was clad in white. The magical combination of the physical processes of reflection and refraction was so hyperphysical that it was glowing as Gold.

I turned back to call Megha but then stopped.

The view inside the room drew perfect symmetry with the view outside. I took a quick glance at the outside and then looked back at my darling lying there on the bed, looking as innocent as a baby with eyes closed, unaware of my presence, with the sunlight falling on her perfectly enough to make the inside view equally hyperphysical.

The mountains were all covered in white; the body was glowing as Gold!

Date: 25th May 2021

Place: ICU Bed No. 28

SpO2: 88

"Go and get Stayfree asap."

Megha hurriedly told with eyes not facing me directly as if trying to hide something. The maid was washing the dishes in the kitchen. I was never required to bring any such stuff earlier, as shopping from Star Bazaar would suffice.

"Me?" I said reluctantly.

"Yes, You." Her voice always had an element of authority, and I loved that.

I got up from the chair, and she came following me to the entrance door. Suddenly, I turned back and held the door.

"Hey, I think I saw a pack there in your wardrobe in the morning."

"Do as I say." and she shut the door in my face.

It was after I had left her and Aarohi at her mom's place in Meerut and stayed alone in Bangalore for almost a year from November 2019 to September 2020, half of which was pre-Covid period, when I realised how many lives she had impacted.

"Didi elli, Bhaiya?" the lady selling the coconuts on the street asked.

I had come for a walk alone after having dinner.

"Didi is in our native; we got a little girl."

She looked happy as she tried to comprehend what I said in Hindi. She replied to me in Kannada, which I did not understand, and then asked me to sit on the nearby bench. She checked two-three coconuts, opened one, put in a straw, and brought it to me.

"I don't have money right now; I just came for a walk."

She again said something in Kannada and started smiling. When she understood that I had not understood, she said,

"Bhot achha."

I thought she was asking if the coconut water was *"bhot achha,"* but just a few seconds later, I realised she was saying,

"Didi bhot achha." and she would start smiling again.

While walking back, I called Megha and told her about this *"bhot achha,"* incident; Megha started laughing as usual.

During our short stay in Indore, we had this security guard in our society who was almost always on night duty. From my interaction with the society members, I learned that he had retired from the army, had come away from his family in Bihar, and was serving as a security guard here. He must be around 58-60 years of age. However, I noticed he always scolded kids playing in the park or riding swings, particularly late in the evening, asking them to return to their homes. It appeared as if the virtues of discipline taught to him in the army were strictly being preached by him, particularly to the kids.

One late night—all three of us—me, Megha, and Aarohi—came out for a walk. It was probably around 10 pm. Aarohi was in her dad's lap while Megha was closely walking when she noticed the same guard having dinner. She was not aware of his background.

"So late?" she casually asked him while walking. The guard gave a serious look, a little confused as to why an unknown lady would ask him such a question.

In the absence of a reply, Megha stopped.

For the colonel of our society, the Brigadier had arrived.

"Why so late, uncle?"

The guard started smiling, seemingly hesitant to answer the question.

"Have your dinner on time, latest by 8 pm."

The Brigadier had passed the orders.

As we walked back to our flat, I told Megha to stay away from that guard, but she just gave me a cute smile in response. I knew my advice had been ignored.

The next night we were again walking when she noticed the same guard disobeying the brigadier's orders.

"Again, late?"

"What to do, Didi? Time passes so quickly."

"But you can plan your work accordingly......"

And then commenced her daily dose of conversation with the guy. He had many stories of his tenure in the army at different and difficult locations, and he just got three pairs of ears to listen to him. All three of us would sit with him for 5-10 minutes to listen to his world of experiences.

Fast forward to 05th June 2021, as Aarohi and I returned home from the hospital, the guy came rushing to our flat as I opened the door on the ringing of the bell. He peeped inside, ignoring me.

"Where is Bitiya?"

I pointed at Aarohi playing inside.

"No... where is Bitiya?"

An intruder into his daily dining schedule had all of a sudden become *bitiya* for him. The guard was left with more number of stories than the number of breathes his *bitiya* was left with.

While these are just three of the many instances, Megha had deeply impacted whosoever she came in touch with.

The lady at the *kirana* store, the milk vendor, the always serious guy at Nandini Milk Parlour, the vegetable vendor, the maids, the car wash guy, the nursing staff in the hospital where Aarohi was born, and the nursing staff in the hospital in Indore, the neighbours, the security personnel, the plumber, the electrician, everyone whom she interacted with, felt a bonding.

She would always be ears to them, learn about their household happenings and their problems, advise them on such matters and ultimately try to make them happy in whichever circumstances they were in. Every maid that worked in our house had a qualifying criterion—

"In which class are your children studying?"

Education, for her, was the panacea to all evils.

At least once a month, she will deliver sermons to the maid on the importance of educating the kids. If, by any chance, the maid came with her daughter to assist her in work, Megha would get annoyed. In less than an hour's interaction with the child, she will fuel her with so much passion that the kid herself would deny working as an assistant to her mom and would prefer going to school.

Anyways, I had brought the Stayfree home. A few days later, she again came rushing and handed me some cash.

"Go and get a Stayfree."

I was panicked this time.

"How many do you use in a month?"

She laughed.

"Go and just get it." she pushed me while opening the main door and kept smiling. She had such a cunning cum shying way of smiling that I always wanted to kiss her.

"Don't run your calculations; just go and get it."

She slammed the door in my face.

I went to the shop and brought what was asked for. Democracy was under real threat in Megha's regime as you could never ask questions but enjoyed whatever Megha did. There was no need to ask her anything because you knew she was all doing it for good.

"Aunty has a daughter." she answered my unasked questions one day.

Megha would start changing their perception; their habits would start changing on their own.

"You cannot force anything on anybody. Even if you do, that won't last long. Change how they perceive the things, make them understand what is right and what is wrong."

She knew the psychology and the process behind habit formation without even reading such books. Master at the art of convincing, she knew how to set things simple and straight.

"They are not bad at heart, none of them. They also have a story; you just have to understand what made them a thief or a criminal and strike at the root cause. Everyone is capable. Do whatever good you can do for them."

Back on the hospital bed…

"No matter what condition a girl is in, these won't stop."

Megha said smilingly while in pain.

"*What?*" I asked inquisitively.

"*Periods.*"

Date: 26th May 2021

Place: ICU Bed No. 28

SpO2: 90

Megha's oxygen level suddenly dropped yesterday, and she was given additional injections. She would prefer lying in prone position as it helped her improve her SpO2 readings and gave rest to her back, for she had been lying on the same bed for the last ten days, not permitted to move.

A girl who never sat at any place for more than 15-20 minutes, preferred doing asanas and yoga kriyas instead of sitting idle, and loved travelling and talking, was tied to the bed with many tubes piercing all through her body.

I would ask my office staff to send some fresh fruits everyday & I would cut them in the morning and put them inside a plastic cup, place tissue over it and then insert a toothpick and take it along with me for Megha whenever I visited the ICU.

But this day, Aarohi was not allowing me to go to the ICU, leaving her alone. Megha was waiting.

"*You love her so much.*" Tears came to her eyes as I wrote ICU Bed No. 28 on the tissue paper and gave the fruit cup to the nurse, asking her to give it to Megha.

"I do." I said as I firmly placed the cup in her hands and got busy playing with Aarohi again.

Only later was I supposed to get to know the reason behind the nurse's tears.

Whenever I sent such stuff through the nursing staff, I would confirm an immediate receipt of the same by Megha on WhatsApp as her phone was with her until now. She would spend the day reading kindle edition of books, playing mantras, and soothing songs to spend the day out.

"How is my kanya?" I saw her message on my WhatsApp.

Sending her a pic of the two of us in the hospital room, I replied,

"Enjoying with the langoora."

"What is the name of our Prime Minister?"

Megha asked it loud as the children looked at her in anticipation. The first to answer the question would get a ten rupees note. There always used to be a lot of bustling among the kids whenever she was about to come up with her next question.

"Everyone is capable. Do whatever small good you can do for them."

And she had her own ways of doing the good. Every Navratri, she will not call the girls in the neighbourhood for *kanya poojan.* Instead, she will ask the maid and her peer maids to bring their kids to our place for *kanya poojan.*

No, do not get her wrong here. Feeding the poor kids wasn't her primary motive here. Navratri gave her an opportunity to double-check the maid's commitment of sending kids to school and also to check if the kids were learning basic things.

"What is the capital of Karnataka?"

It was as if she was the Amitabh Bachchan of *Kaun Banega Crorepati.* She would hand over a ten rupees note to the child who answered the question first. The kids will also enjoy the game. While I have seen kids running from one home to another on *kanya poojan* in the lure of *prasadam* or money, the same kids would spend almost an hour at our home answering her questions. Ultimately, she will distribute Navratri gifts among all kids taking commitments of what percentage of marks they will secure in their examinations.

But what did I do during this process?

Yes, I first enjoyed watching my *kanya* while she played her quiz game with the kids. Secondly, I was also tasked with shooting the entire one-hour episode of this *Kaun Banega Crorepati* on her mobile phone. She was super excited about photographs and videos.

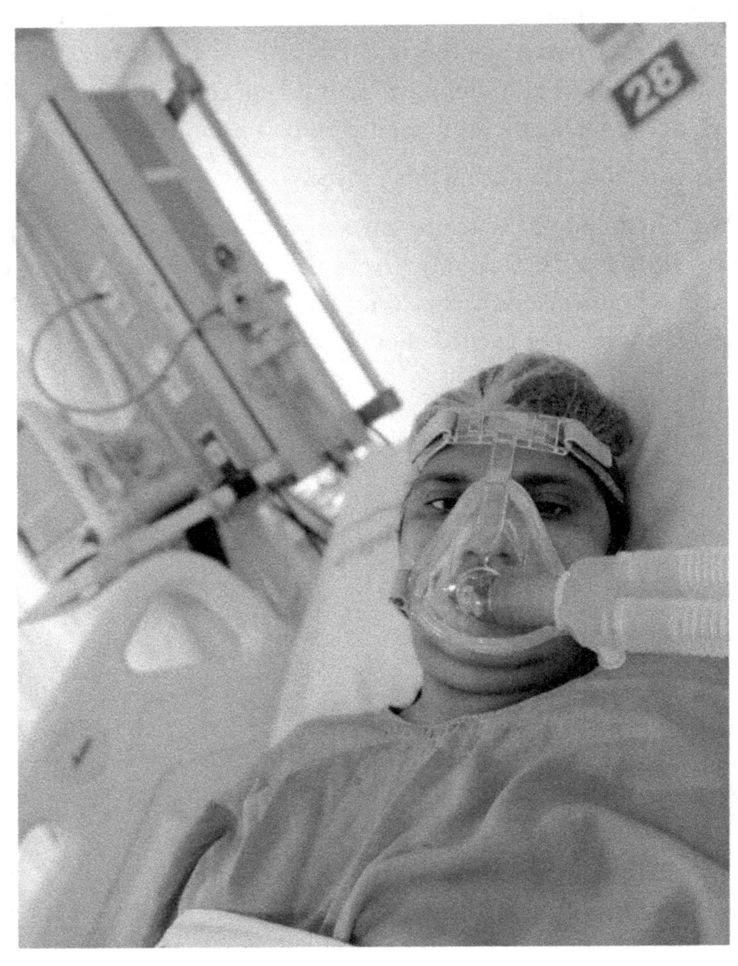

A selfie taken by Megha on 26th May 2021

Date: 27th May 2021

Place: ICU Bed No. 28

SpO2: 88

"How many days more, Ankur? I want to go out, breathe fresh air, travel with Aarohi, and enjoy your morning tea."

"Goa chalein?" we were reading the newspaper on the dining table while sipping morning tea. I was excited about her Goan idea.

"Yes." I answered casually, my eyes still going through the newspaper headlines. By the way, who says no to Goa?

"To chalo, let's go!"

I coughed and spilt tea on the newspaper as she stood up from her chair, suddenly saying so.

"When?" I asked, trying to control my coughing.

"Right now!"

No flight arrangements, no hotel bookings, no beachwears, no advance preparations, and here we were, lying on the upper berth of an AC sleeper bus from Bangalore to Goa the same evening. It was fun calling the office and telling them I won't be able to come for a week without telling them anything about our sudden escapades.

"Always go off the beaten track."

She was always like a *"Aaj kucch toofani karte hain"* sort of girl.

As we lay together on the berth of the AC bus, I asked,

"Where should we stay in Goa-Taj or..."

"Check out a simple beachside shack or cottage for a stay."

I had some Taj vouchers from Amex with me and thought it would be financially prudent to timely exhaust them as they could have provided us a free 2-3 days of stay, but she was always ready with her own plans as if she was always going by her reflexes and not by in-depth deliberations.

"Book only for one night." she added.

Now I looked at her with grave seriousness, pissed off by her one-night program.

"One night? Are we returning tomorrow?"

"No, we would stay in a new beach side cottage every day."

The bus reached Goa the next morning. We hired an Activa from near the bus stand itself, put in the single cabin-sized trolly bag in the leg space of the Activa where it exactly fitted, and then we measured the entire length and breadth of Goa on this Activa for the next five days, dropping it back at the same location and boarding the return bus from Goa to Bangalore. This sudden, completely unplanned trip with just two of us together was one of the finest trips we had ever made.

And if you think that this was an isolated case of an unplanned trip, then you are wrong. We were habitual of escaping the daily cobwebs of life like this; otherwise, travelling thirty-six cities across India in our first thirty-six months of marriage could never have been possible.

One fine night, Megha made a similar plan to visit Gokarna on Christmas. In the morning, we were driving the car with one of her friends and her husband sitting in the rear seat, me driving the car, and Megha seated in the co-driver seat, only to find that no rooms were available in the entire Gokarna on the eve of Christmas. We spent half of the night lying on the seaside of Half Moon Beach at Gokarna, and only when the high tides started dripping our feet, did we rush to our car to spend the rest of the night inside it.

Not only this, once we started for Mysore with her sister and her kids with an intent to return by late night, but after reaching Mysore, she planned for Ooty, after reaching Ooty, she planned for Coonnoor, and though she had further plans, we ran short of clothes as we had been travelling wearing the same set for the past five days!

"How many more days, Ankur?"

I did not know she was asking for the number of days she would spend in the hospital bed or the number of days she was left with!

Date: 28th May 2021

Place: ICU Bed No. 28

SpO2: 89

"One water bottle

Two glasses

One Mewa Mix

One comb

One coconut oil."

I had sent these items to her bed in the ICU on her demand. She had her own standards of hygiene, and she had asked for a separate water bottle with disposable glasses. I loved how I found the home when I returned from the office on alternate Saturdays, which used to be off for her but working for me as the flat would be glistening. Clothes will be orderly placed in my wardrobe. She would spend the entire day cleaning the rooms and ensure that the walls speak of exuberance.

On the alternate Saturdays, which would be off for me too, I would join hands with her—cleaning the house and getting dirty—spending the afternoon watching a movie on the TV in our bedroom in each other's arms.

Life cannot be more perfect!

"Look at my hair." I noticed she looked fresh, her hair neatly tied up, a little soaked in coconut oil.

"Didi washed my hair."

I looked at the nurse, who smiled at us, acknowledging her admiration.

"Ankur, I have a request."

I was in the office when I got this call from her sister. She sounded serious. I got up from my chair and exited my cabin to find a place away from the office staff and the general public.

"Tell me, Didi."

"Bring her a dishwasher."

"A dishwasher?"

"Yes, I think she is overloaded with work."

"What happened? There are just three of us in the house in Indore. Why a dishwasher?"

"No, I feel that she is taking a lot of pain, handling daily chores from morning till evening, the maids aren't coming due to Covid, and she is also working from home for her office and taking care of Aarohi all on her own. She appears overburdened."

"Did Megha ask you to ask me for a dishwasher?"

I grew a little serious and anxious as Megha and I were so bonded to each other that no communication was required to reach us from any outsider, not even her sister. Had Megha asked for one dishwasher, I would have ordered two and ensured they reached the same day.

"No, No Ankur. She will infact get annoyed if she learns about your plans to order a dishwasher. You know how thrift she is."

"Alright, Didi, any specific choice?"

"I will send you links on WhatsApp."

The dishwasher was delivered on the expected date but could never wash the dishes, for there remained unknown sins of the past to be washed off first.

Date: 29th May 2021

Place: ICU Bed No. 28

SpO2: 90

"We will continue staying here only."

"But you have tested Covid negative today; you cannot stay in a Covid ward."

"What about Aarohi? We have not done the test for her yet. I don't know anything; I will stay with Megha, either in the ICU or in any room."

The floor in charge on the other side sighed, thinking that I had placed the receiver.

"Ye aise nahi jayega." I heard the doctor's voice, who might probably be sitting there on the floor incharge's cabin seeing the documents of my discharge.

A few moments later—Aarohi & I were shifted to a private room. At times, when I will not be able to visit the ICU because of Aarohi, I would use the landline phone in the room to call ICU to get to know her parameters. By this time, Aarohi had learnt that this landline phone equipment was meant for getting connected with her mom. Infact, till date, whenever she sees a landline phone in any of the hotel rooms we visit, she picks the receiver up, saying, *"Hello, Mumma!"*

She was not sleeping at all that night. It was already 2 am. I was trying to discuss things with some known and unknown doctors in the US and Canada, but Aarohi would snatch the phone off my hands. She probably got bored of Masha and the Bear that kept coming repetitively on the TV. Her drawing books were full, the notebook we had brought for Aarohi was filled with the sketched outlines of her hand. Megha had taught her to keep her hand on the notebook and draw the outlines with the sketch pen.

I had not slept for days and nights together, and as I took the phone back from Aarohi's hands, she started crying. As I tried to manage things, Aarohi grew crankier and started crying at the top of her voice.

None of the tricks worked, I tried taking her in my lap, but she kicked; I tried showing her TV, but she continued; I attempted acting like the bear of Masha but failed, and by this time, Aarohi, as her name suggests, had ascended to the highest of the notes she could strike while crying. It was 02:30 am by now. The nurses started knocking on the door, wondering what had happened, and even their efforts to convince Aarohi failed.

As I tried consoling her, Aarohi pulled the tube attached to the IV drip on my hand, and it came out straight off my skin—a bright red vertical line with blood oozing out of it—came up on my hand running from the wrist towards the fingers. The nurse hurried up and placed some cotton over it, which soon turned red. She brought another piece of cotton, and this too, turned red. She called another nurse for help but two more cotton pieces turned red.

I wondered why the blood was not clotting and it was only when the second nurse realised I was on blood thinners as part of the Covid treatment that she gave me some medicine and put some spray on my hand.

The blood stopped oozing; Aarohi stopped crying!

Date: 30th May 2021

Place: ICU Bed No. 28

SpO2: 90

"Ankur, I got a call from the accounts department."

"Accounts department?" I wondered why the accounts department of the hospital would call Megha.

"They said some dues are pending for settlement."

"I will speak to them."

"Do you need money?"

"I need you!"

1st of April every year, we almost had an off on account of the annual closing. This was the day when both of us would sit together, open Microsoft Excel on my laptop and plan the entire financial year on the very first day of the year. By the 2nd of April, all our debt-oriented investments would be made while the rest 363 days would be meant for equity investing. One thing she was very serious about was money.

"It's not just money. It is the value of the efforts you have put in, the pain you have taken. Value its value."

While I was a complete spendthrift, Megha was very particular about spending habits. If you are a lady reading this book, no matter whether you are working or a housewife, this is the most important trait of her that you need to inculcate.

Men, by nature, tend to spend extravagantly. A woman, who a man loves beyond limits, can only exercise restraint on his spending habits. If you are not able to do so, that means either you are unwilling to exercise restraint and love indulging in the extravaganza, or it means that the man doesn't love you enough. In both cases, you are sending an invitation to disaster—both financially and personally.

I have many friends who though, are Vice Presidents and Executives Directors in hot shot investment banks drawing lakhs and crores in salary as CTC but unable to run even small ticket SIPs for them or their kids' future. Even if they do so, their mutual funds' corpus is the first thing they would rely on in case of any exigency, travel plan, domestic need, medical emergency or a family function. The things are quite clear. They run and are still running from paycheck to paycheck and for any reason, in case the pay check gets delayed for a month, their credit card dues would bring them on roads. Despite attaining the maximum requisite qualification for earning money, they lack the minimum requisite commonsense for spending money. They never feel shy about contacting you to borrow money to meet their ever-growing consumption requirements.

Megha would feel pained to hear if someone would quote money as a problem in frequent tours and travel. She had the quota fixed for every aspect of life. No compromise on lifestyle with a disciplined approach towards investing and further strict control over spending habits was a perfect blend, and that is what is essential for every couple to make their financial life blissful enough.

Whenever a discussion on money broke out in any event with friends or colleagues, she would proudly submit,

"Ankur is my investment banker and I am his Relationship Manager." and would wink looking at me.

One thing she hated was learned women sitting idly at home as housewives.

"Why do you need a degree if you have to sit at home as a child-producing machine? Why shouldn't you contribute actively to the country's GDP? Unless women participate in learning and earning and have fair asset ownership in their names, they will always depend on males. Social freedom comes from financial freedom."

Her rule was simple,

"Study what you love, do what you study, enjoy what you do!"

"Why don't you educate people on personal finance?" she asked me inquisitively one day.

"Sounds like a nice idea!" I replied.

She placed the mobile phone in the landscape position in the kitchen, opened the camera and pressed the video button. For her, life was instant.

"What are you doing?"

"I will ask you finance questions, you answer and we will record them."

"Hahaha..." I laughed out loud as she continued capturing the smiles.

"Tell me, Mr. Saxena" she asked while turning the camera towards me, trying to fit in the picture frame, *"what shall be the name of the show?"*

"Cosy Couple's Conundrums!" I replied, laughing my heart out.

I started writing a series of blogs titled *"Dear Aarohi"* to motivate young parents to plan a future for their children.

As a parent, she said, every young couple would like to learn the art and science of investment—if not for themselves, at least for their children.

For any of you interested in investments, I have the smallest yet complete, just a 4-point financial plan, to which Megha added the 5th point.

1. Get a plain vanilla term plan.
2. Get adequate health insurance cover.
3. Ensure you have an emergency corpus—partly in FDs and partly in debt-oriented mutual funds.
4. Invest the rest of everything in equities—not direct stocks if you are a novice, but equity mutual funds.
5. ***Make sure you enjoy life at every moment.***

Financial Planning is NOT about reaching a designated digit mark by sacrificing all joys of life. It is about enjoying the life in the present without sacrificing the future.

Date: 31st May 2021

Place: ICU Bed No. 28

SpO2: 89

The wickets were falling every now and then, not in any cricket match but on the beds in the ICU. While the doctors were giving their 200%, Covid virus was not showing any mercy. We had become habitual of seeing one to two departures every day. I would console Megha to stay positive as she was the only one in the ICU conscious and talking while almost all other patients were on ventilator support.

"What a waste?" she said in disappointment. I looked at her for further insights into what prompted her to say so.

"People are dying outside because of oxygen shortage, and here, patients getting oxygen support are also dying. The doctors' efforts are also going waste despite risking their own lives."

One thing she always hated was wastage. You will invite her wrath if you leave anything unfinished on your dinner plate.

"Khao man bhar, chhodo na kan bhar." was Megha's driving motto when it came to food consumption.

One night it happened that Megha prepared Colocasia, and I found one, a little uncooked or raw, and left it on my plate. As I got up from the dinner table, she noticed the piece of *Arabi* lying on my plate.

"Give that to me."

"It's raw."

"I have teeth."

"Ohhoo... it's just one."

"I have thirty-two. Give that to me."

In the heat of the moment, I gobbled it up in my mouth, making unpleasant expressions saying,

"I, too, have teeth."

Yet another thing she disliked was people's attitude towards cleanliness. She had her own *"Swachhta Abhiyan"* always under progress.

One Diwali, she asked me to book Rajdhani train tickets against a usual flight from Bangalore to Delhi. Reiterating, I must admit that this tiring and long train journey is another memorable experience of travelling with her. The fact, why I am mentioning the train journey is because what ensued was more interesting than the train journey.

After reaching Delhi, Megha asked to take an auto from Hazrat Nizamuddin Railway Station to Anand Vihar Bus Stand, from where she wanted to travel in a bus to Meerut.

But this poor auto driver committed the mistake of spitting on the road while driving. It was around 6 in the morning. The sermons ensued, and I could see the auto driver gulping the entire pan masala risking his life with cancer but couldn't dare spitting on the road again. It wasn't just serious scolding that she used to instruct the other fellow on what was right and what was wrong, but she would bring in an element of sensitivity and responsibility in her advice that will not only have an immediate effect but also leave an a long-lasting impact on such behavioural misadventures.

Our trip to Andamans witnessed another such incident when while waiting for entry into the Jarwas area for an onward visit to one island, the passengers had come out of their taxis that formed a queue on the road waiting for the gate to open when one of the family in a Thar threw plastic plates and other stuff on the roadside from the car's window just a few metres away from where we were having tea in a tea stall.

Megha stood up. So did I. Both of us reached the front of this car, and just her angry looks were strong enough to convey the message to the travellers inside of what mistake they had committed. The tea vendors also came out from the stalls and started screaming at them in their native language. The family's kids inside the car were told to go down and pick up everything they had thrown on the street and put it in the dustbin.

"Kids learn almost everything from their parents, be better!"

Back in the hospital, we stood hopeful of turning the tides in our favour, without knowing what waste all the efforts would result in a few days later!

Date: 01st June 2021

Place: ICU Bed No. 28

SpO2: 91

"*What are you doing here?*" she asked me as I came to the ICU to see her.

"*Why don't you go home? Aarohi is also suffering here. Call Mom to Indore; things will be better, at least for Aarohi, once my mom comes.*"

My parents had been Covid positive in Meerut for the last 30-40 days. Repetitive RTPCRs were done to check if someone could fly to Indore, but it was like God did not want anybody to come to us for us to keep suffering on our own.

While my sister tried coming to Indore and she even had booked flights, I rejected her proposal as; first, they too had been recently hospitalised for Covid, and calling them to Indore would mean putting them at risk again, and second, their arrival would require Aarohi and me to move out of the hospital placing once a day limit on me meeting Megha. I did not want to leave her alone. Rather, if the doctors would permit, I would prefer staying with Megha 24*7.

Further, if anybody came to Indore, they would also stand at risk of getting infected as I would be visiting the hospital's Covid ward every day and I did not want any more trouble.

"Take 15 days leave from office."

"15 days?"

"Yes, 15 days. The second wave is getting severe day by day."

"But Megha, I am heading one of the biggest branches in Indore. There is a lot of work pending. And what if the boss himself goes on leave? What would the other staff members think?"

"You are thinking about what they will think. Why don't you think about Aarohi? It is just a matter of 15 days."

"15 days is a very long period Megha. The leave will not be granted."

"Don't request for leave; just take it."

"You know government schemes are going on. The Collector calls me daily to his office for updates."

"Are you worried about your salary?"

"Not at all."

"Listen, I am working from home. You might not get paid for 15-20 days, but that's okay. I am here. Let us go to our village. You play with Aarohi and enjoy your full time with her while I will continue working from home."

It was exactly on the 15th day of this conversation that I had brought the virus home.

Date: 02nd June 2021

Place: ICU Bed No. 28

SpO2: 90

"I can feel my heart sinking."

I saw her message on WhatsApp and rushed to ICU, asking the floor attendant to take care of Aarohi. The entire hospital staff had become a family to us by now. Add to it Aarohi's tantrums; she had become the darling of every person working in the hospital. Infact, one guy working with NTPC came to us at the time of his discharge from the hospital.

"Thank You, Aarohi."

Aarohi won't let anyone touch her cheeks. Social distancing had become the new norm for babies during this Covid regime, and Aarohi's mother had taught her well on this.

He looked at me with teary eyes.

"I want to tell you that Aarohi gave me a new life. I was on oxygen support for so many days, broken from the inside, wondering if I could ever meet my daughters again. But Aarohi's voice reminded me of Meera and Myra—I was missing them so badly. Aarohi made me hold on to life. Thank you once again."

He came thrice to meet Aarohi before finally checking out his room.

I had reached ICU only to find nurses moving quickly towards and away from her bed. Megha was being given emergency medication to revive her to normalcy. She had her eyes closed.

I felt I required strength to keep standing. My legs shivered. I felt I would vomit.

"Megha!" my voice broke.

And she opened her eyes. It was painful to see her in this state.

"I am okay."

I took a sigh of relief. The nurses had completed the course of injections to be given to her and allowed us to sit together for a while.

"You know, it is not the pain on the left side of your chest which people think is a heart attack. Your entire chest sags, particularly the area below the throat, as if the entire machinery is stopping."

"It's okay, Megha; you are up and speaking; forget about it."

She smiled and looked at the 4th bed on her left. The old lady who was on ventilator support was not there.

"Departed?" I asked.

"No, discharged."

"Really?"

"Yes, she woke up, and doctors removed her from ventilator support. She was stable and might have been shifted to a normal room."

"That's good news, Megha. If she could do it at this stage, you are much stronger. We would get shifted to a normal room soon. Don't worry."

Megha nodded in affirmation.

Date: 03rd June 2021

Place: ICU Bed No. 28

SpO2: 85

No matter how worse the situation might be, Megha had a permanent smile affixed to her face. I had grown agnostic, visiting ICU and staring at her SpO2 reading on screen. I could feel chills running down my spine when I raised my eyes to look at her SpO2 levels. I wanted her back the way she was just 22 days back.

"Can you see something here?" she touched her throat area, and I could see some swelling on her throat and upper chest.

"Yes, but what's that?"

"I had heard of cheese burst so far; today, I got to know that lungs also burst."

I stood up impatiently as if something had burst inside me. I called the nurses immediately to get to know what Megha was talking about.

"The lungs at times get ruptured due to which oxygen gets accumulated near the windpipe." the nurse told.

I did not know who to slap or who to kill. It was as if the villain in our love story was not visible and things were not turning in our favour at all.

Megha smiled at my helplessness.

"There is more to it."

I stood up again more impatiently, with added helplessness.

Things were falling apart and I was not able to make them better.

"Look at my nose."

It was covered under the oxygen mask but since that was transparent, I could still see red marks all around her nose."

"And what's that?"

"I have been on oxygen support for last so many days; this chilling flow of air has caused blood to freeze inside my nose. They just removed some 20-30 grams of blood clots from my nose a few minutes back. The only good thing is that I feel comparatively less congestion while breathing now."

Megha was put on HFNC + NRBM support for some time as continuous bipap deployment had made her nose stiff and air bubbles had formed in her throat passage as the doctors suspected leakage from the lungs. It had become a never-ending torture to her. Every breath she took in, would bruise her nose and chest.

"Do you know oxygen actually kills?"

I thought she was talking about the black fungus, for she had been telling the new incidents one by one in quick succession. But she had turned the mood hyperphysical by now.

"Breathe in." she asked.

"Who?"

"You, who else?"

"Oh, Come on, Megha, not here?"

"I said breathe in."

I was used to going by whatever she said.

"Take a deep breath."

I closed my eyes while sitting by her side in the ICU and breathed in.

"Now hold it for a while, and yes, now breathe out."

I followed her steps thrice and then opened my eyes.

"Enough."

"No, wait, tell me which was more comfortable?"

"Which what?"

"Which was more comfortable—breathing in or breathing out?"

Ahhhaa... I was caught. She was correct. I had also felt this earlier while doing power yoga sessions with her.

While inhaling and holding breath would cause a lot of anxiety, and the muscles would get a little tense, it was breathing this air out, which would relax the body. I never knew she was practically doing this research here, on her own body, on each of her breath.

"Come on, tell me."

"Breathing out." I confirmed.

"Exactly." she snapped with the SpO2 device stuck to her fingers.

"And look at me; probably, I am not able to relax."

"Means?"

"This oxygen mask is throwing cool air inside my nose with heavy pressure. They just want the air to somehow reach my lungs with this pressure but what about exhalation? May be the body does not need this much air or may be this much air pressure."

"The doctors are professionals; they know these things better."

"I am not questioning their expertise. But do you realise that the primary work of lungs is not to inhale oxygen but to exhale carbon dioxide from the body so that it can relax?"

"The doctor has called you in his chamber." the nurse told me as I was moving out of the ICU. Her tone added worry to my already tense state of mind. It was like I could breathe in, but the things were getting choked somewhere inside and I could not breathe out.

The doctor drew a complete textbook diagram of the lungs in

front of me.

"Look here."

He pointed at the entry point where the windpipe was meeting the lungs.

"There is no problem till this point. The oxygen is getting delivered to where it should be."

"Then where is the problem?"

He moved the pen point to the tubes running away from the lungs towards the heart.

"The problem lies here."

I looked at the doctor, unable to understand what he was trying to convey.

"The lungs are like thin membranes, just like a thin polythene bag. What happens to such a polythene bag when it gets soaked in water?"

"It sticks. I mean, the sides get stuck to each other."

"Exactly, this is what has happened." the doctor confirmed my hypothesis.

"The lungs are able to get the oxygen, but they are not able to exchange it with the carbon dioxide as the tubes on the other side are affected by Covid induced pneumonia."

"You mean the membranes on the other side of the lungs are stuck with each other exactly like a thin polythene bag?"

"Yes, the exchange of O2 and CO2 is not happening effectively. This is what we call lung fibrosis-induced ARD in medical terminology, where ARD stands for Acute Respiratory Distress Syndrome, and there is no treatment for this. As such, her SpO2 levels look okay, but her blood pO2 levels are declining, as evident from the ABG (Arterial Blood Gas) test we are doing almost twice daily."

The doctor was telling exactly what Megha was experiencing!

Date: 04th June 2021

Place: ICU Bed No. 28

SpO2: 86

"Mom is coming."

You could easily notice the happiness on her face the moment I announced that her mom was coming to Indore. The only point of worry was that no test was done for Aarohi to check if she had turned Covid negative yet and Aarohi was supposed to stay at home with Megha's Mom.

Were we taking an additional risk? But why would I take any such step as I had been handling everything on my own for so many days? What prompted me to decide to get yet another life at risk without knowing whether Aarohi was Covid negative?

"If possible, call your parents here." The doctor concluded while wrapping up the piece of paper on which he had drawn the diagram of the lungs.

"Is she at risk?"

"I have seen many patients recovering even after more serious condition than this. Have faith."

I broke down in his chamber, completely begging for her life. Things were changing so rapidly for the worse. And I was not able to do anything to safeguard her from the jaws of death. It was a cruel duel between love and destiny, and I knew my love was much stronger. It was just that the thin line of probability was getting thinner.

"Ankur, take me home. I am not able to bear anymore." her WhatsApp message flashed on my screen.

She was not aware of what situation we had entered. She just knew she has to hold on, and with every passing second, every breathe going in and out, the lungs would heal on their own. It was just a matter of time.

But the game had just begun.

"Send me a notebook and a pen." Yet another message popped up on my phone's screen.

"Reaching in two minutes." I responded.

I gave her a pen and Aarohi's notebook on which she had drawn the sketch of her hand. The next few hours were crucial. After going through her parameters and readings, I rang up numerous doctors, all of whom sounded low.

In the family, everybody was already in panic for the wait had been so long, but things had not improved.

Aarohi tested Covid negative on 04th night!

Date: 05th June 2021

Place: ICU Bed No. 28

SpO2: 90

"Tell me, what was there in her hands?"

I WhatsApp-ed her late at night, but it must have been daytime in the United States of America. She was one of Megha's best friends who knew palmistry.

It was the fourth year in our college. Campus placements used to start by the second half of 3rd year in those days. While I was already campus placed in Wipro, Megha was still looking for a job opportunity. Both of us were in the same college, same branch. That's a long story for which we can allocate a separate time-space, but here, we all were going to Lucknow by Nauchandi Express that night, Megha as a placement aspirant and I as the placement coordinator. Everybody knew I was travelling because of Megha. The coach was full with students of our college.

She was also one of them when on the running train, she revealed she could read hands. And then it was like all the passengers on the train, known or unknown, wanted to know their future. Palm after palm after palm, her palmistry was being put to test. Before she could conclude her palmistry session, Megha finally came ahead, unfolding her palm in her lap.

"Maate, tell me something about my future." Megha giggled in her usual style as I watched the conundrums from the berth above.

She looked at the lines on her hand for quite some time. So far, for me, it was like a person fooling another person as I did not believe in any such stuff.

"Have you ever fallen sick?" she asked, her eyes still fixed on her hand.

"What sort of question is this?" Megha kept giggling in her style, placing another hand in front of her mouth and laughing, *"Fever and cold is a usual phenomenon; everybody falls sick."*

She grew more serious reading her hand. The coach, which was buzzing with the Ho Ha of the college kids, had gone silent all of a sudden as she peeped more into her hands. Only the sound of the train running on the railway track could be heard during this silence.

"No, I mean, have you ever been in a life-threatening health condition?"

I got up from my berth and came down, sitting beside Megha, trying to read out what she was reading, seeing her hand.

"Tell me, what is there in her hands?" I inquired.

She raised her head, looking at both of us together.

"Her lifeline is broken!"

"Tell me, what was there in her hands?"

"Oh, man, she will be fine, Ankur. Sending all my prayers."

"No, I want to know will the lines meet. What is the significance of the second half of the lifeline?"

"Don't worry, I know it's difficult, but she will be fine."

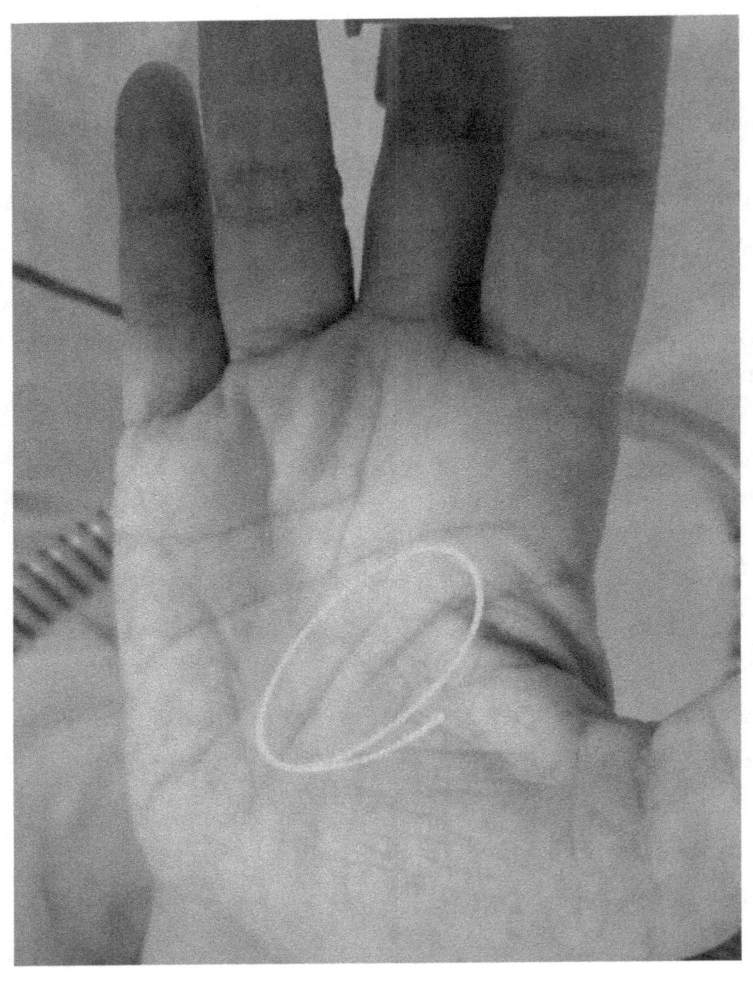

Megha's hand: Never knew these lines

could be this significant

I reached ICU at the usual 4 pm, the second time in the day. The doctor was on round and was discussing things with the nursing staff in front of Megha's bed. I went inside and checked Megha. She appeared okay. The nurse later told me that the doctor was waiting outside for me. Without letting Megha know about this, I came out to see the doctor.

"We need to take her on the ventilator."

I was perturbed hearing the word—*"ventilator."*

"Ventilator? But why?"

"Her condition warrants so."

"But she is fine, up and speaking, alive, conscious. Why a ventilator?"

"Her blood pO2 levels are continuously declining with no signs of improvement."

"So what?"

"Any of her organs might fail in the absence of proper oxygen supply to them, the heart goes first generally in such cases."

Her words struck me hard at this moment...

"I can feel my heart sinking."

I shivered with fear.

"What if we don't opt for a ventilator?"

"Choice is yours; in both the cases, she has only 1% chance of survival."

"Survival?" I was so far thinking that we were struggling for recuperation; I never knew when the ordeal turned into a fight for survival!

"Choice is yours; in both the cases, she has only 1% chance of survival."

His words kept buzzing in my head as I came down from ICU to the ground floor and sat on the empty bench, holding my head with both hands.

"Only 1% chance of survival."

This was totally against the mathematical conclusion of a 1% probability of death due to Covid we discussed at the beginning of this book. I never knew when we fell into this 1% bucket with 99% accuracy.

"Only 1% chance of survival."

The words kept hitting me repeatedly. I tried controlling myself, but the words kept echoing...

"Only 1% chance of survival."

I breathed in and then breathed out. It appeared as if every breath was an insult to Megha, a mockery of her worsening situation.

"Only 1% chance of survival."

How will I tell this to Megha?

"Only 1% chance of survival."

How do I convince her for ventilator?

She was alive, conscious, speaking, eating, and overall staying strong. Why a ventilator?

"Only 1% chance of survival."

How do I tell this to her?

Exactly now, a WhatsApp message flashed on my screen,

"Ankur, come fast."

I fell on the floor once while running and then fell twice.

She was in ultimate pain. The pain was emanating from her spine. The nurses were rubbing iodex on her back, but Megha was smiling in discomfort.

"This is not stopping at all, Ankur."

I started massaging her back with my hands. The nurse's expressions told me that it wasn't going to work. The iodex was just a placebo.

I had given her DRDO's 2DG medicine a few hours earlier, but the oxygen levels had not improved.

Aarohi and I were discharged from the hospital. Her Mom had arrived at our home. I left Aarohi with her Nani and rushed towards the hospital with her mom-made *halwa.*

The glow in her eyes could be easily noticed while having *halwa.* After a long span of almost 20 days, she was having something other than the hospital food.

"My Mom is the best cook; everything she prepares tastes like amrit." She told every nurse, offering *halwa* to them.

Even this *amrit* could not grant her life!

Date: 06th June 2021

Place: ICU Bed No. 28

SpO2: 75

"On the way with Aloo Parantha."

I texted her in the morning, as she sent me a message stating that the SpO2 levels had fallen to 60s and she was being shifted from HFNC + NRBM combination to Venti-BIPAP again. I tried diverting her mind by the time I reached her by disclosing the breakfast menu.

"You have 24 hours to decide."

The doctor's words echoed as I drove the car to the hospital. With each tick of the clock, she was getting away from me. After bringing lunch from home to her, I sat on the same bench on the ground floor where I sat yesterday. It had started raining heavily.

Hundreds of calls with hundreds of doctors in the last 24 hours had confirmed that she needed a full-fledged ventilator support, which required placing tubes into her mouth down to her trachea to enable the oxygen to flow down to her lungs. Her nasal passage was henceforth required to be used for delivering food in the form of liquid to her food pipe and she will remain unconscious till the time her lungs start responding on their own. No more talks, no more conversations, no more WhatsApp, no more homemade food, no more visits to the ICU, leaving everything to the game of probability and all this at the cost of not knowing if she would ever regain consciousness. But there was no way out.

What if I say no to the ventilator?

She would die in a flash; any of her organs would fail at any time. The blood was carrying only one-third of the requisite amount of oxygen, which meant that her organs were oxygen starved. She had already felt her heart sinking just a few days back. Maybe she had already had a heart attack but somehow survived. What if it recurs?

"Choice is yours; in both the cases, she has only 1% chance of survival."

It was as if the time was ticking but I wasn't able to arrive at a decision.

But the choice was to be made; there was no other choice. If you did not choose the ventilator, you were choosing an organ failure. There was no way out. Her lungs were not responding.

"You know, trees are the lungs of the planet." she said while planting two Ashoka trees in our garden just outside our home in Meerut. It was our second Diwali at home after marriage as we flew from Bangalore to Delhi on the festive occasion.

It was 04th of June 2017 when she murmured in my ears on that lazy Sunday as I was sleeping. It was 5 in the morning in Bangalore.

"Let's go. Get Up, Ankur."

I opened my eyes. Usually, I was the one who would wake up early.

"What happened?"

"Just get ready. We are going out."

I looked at the clock. The sun hadn't risen yet, and it was partially dark outside.

"Where?"

"Just get up and get dressed. Wear something old but comfortable. You have to plough 36 acres of land today."

Sleep ran off my eyes as ploughing 36 acres of land hit my ears. It was usual for me to be woken up with such surprises at times and I loved how mysteriously and mischievously she would spell things out for me.

"And we will go by bike, not by car."

She had her own choices whenever we went for long drives.... a..a...a.. long rides!

We rode for around 25 km to reach Bommasandra from Koramangala. Hundreds of people had gathered there for this "Forest in the City" campaign organised by Sansera Foundation. It appeared to be a herculean task of planting thousands of saplings in an area spread over 36 acres of land. But it was here that I realised the power of community because as we took up the shovel, dug the earth up, and planted the 5th sapling, we found the entire 36 acres of land covered with greenery.

Now those three hours could have been utilised for anything else—an overdose of sleep, reading books or newspapers or watching a movie but the satisfaction that drove in after these three hours was beyond comparison; the day concluded with a group photograph when the camera flashes turned on and all the people screamed, not "Say Cheese" but "Say Trees!"

Megha had given several lungs to the planet; her very own lungs were not responding!

It was as if the time had stopped, and the day seemed to be a decade.

"Choice is yours; in both the cases, she has only 1% chance of survival."

It was just seven years to our marriage. Aarohi had just come into our family. We had a whole lot of dreams, whole lot of plans, and here I was, sitting to decide what to choose with the same percentage of probability.

"Choice is yours; in both the cases, she has only 1% chance of survival."

And I had not arrived at a decision yet. Why do I have to take the decision? It was her life. Why shouldn't Megha be informed about the situation? We haven't hidden anything from each other since we met in college. Life had been wonderful after that, with no complaints at all.

But how do I tell her she had just a 1% chance of survival and that it was not a choice? It was a fight between 99% of chances of dying in a flash and 99% chances of dying a slow death. Where was life in this choice? How do I tell this to her?

The rain had stopped. It was 06:34 pm when Megha's message flashed on my WhatsApp.

"Spend some time with me; that's the only choice we are left with."

I cried so loud that the entire hospital staff and the public rushed towards me. Gathering courage, I ran to Megha wiping tears from my eyes.

I entered smilingly inside the ICU, trying not to reveal my state of helplessness.

"How is my girl now?" I asked her.

"Not good."

"Why? You are my strength Megha and you have been fighting so well; things are under control and improving."

"I am not able to eat."

"Means?"

"They are saying that as they remove the mask from my face so that I can eat, the oxygen levels are dropping."

I immediately called the nurse and enquired.

"The doctor must have told you about this already." she said while trying to look away from Megha and me. In the last 20 days of our stay in the hospital, the entire staff had become a family to us. I didn't know whether she tried to hide her tears or hide the fact that Megha had just 1% chance of survival.

"Okay, give it to me; I will feed her with my hands."

She brought the tiffin box I had brought in the afternoon. There was still some parantha left in it.

"Okay, Megha, Open your mouth."

Megha lifted the oxygen mask up with her hands and opened her mouth. I brought my hand with parantha in it near her face with my eyes stuck on the readings on the screen behind her.

80....

70....

60....

50....

40....

30....

Before Megha could take the piece in her mouth, she wore her oxygen mask back and gasped. I felt tremors inside. Megha could not take the bite and preferred wearing the mask in a flash. Her SpO2 levels started rising once again...

30...

40...

50...

60...

72...

75...

I looked at her. The nurse looked at both of us and left.

"Should I give it one more try?" I felt choked, as if my SpO2 levels had dropped simultaneously.

Megha responded in negative. She was not able to eat.

I looked at her from top to bottom. Everything was intact. Her breezy hair, her voracious eyes, her lips with a small black mole exactly above the mid of the upper lip, a perfectly curated body well maintained to the height of aesthetics. Yet she was not able to breathe.

What was happening inside her?

Why was it happening to her?

I called the nurse back.

"We will go for intubation."

"Okay, I will bring the consent form."

The nurse left while Megha stared at me, puzzled.

"Look, Megha." I gave my best attempt to tell her things calmly without an inch of me letting her know what I knew.

"The doctor has suggested intubation for you."

I had deliberately chosen the medical terminology of intubation for her as talking about the ventilator would spill the beans.

"And what is that?"

"Since you are not able to eat on your own, they will use the nasal passage to deliver food to your body in liquid form, and during this process, you will be partly unconscious though you will be able to hear and respond."

"Is that really required?"

"It is just to ensure that your body gets food timely."

She looked around and pointed at an almost 80 years old lady on similar support. May be, from this distance, she did not notice the ventilator tubes going into her throat.

"You mean just like that?"

I nodded in affirmation.

"Okay, do as the doctor has advised, don't worry."

I felt like breaking down completely. It was as if I would get a heart attack before her.

And then were the beans spilt.

Two of the nurses came rushing to us as I stood by the side of her bed in the ICU. Tears rolled down their cheeks as they asked me,

"Bhaiya, why did you choose intubation?"

They had got to know this from the nurse who had gone to bring the consent form.

Megha & I looked puzzled; Megha—because she wondered why the nurse would cry at her getting intubated, which just meant only a mode of food delivery to her in a semiconscious state, and I—because that was what was advised by the doctor. Was there any catch?

"Nobody has come back after that." the nurses continued as tears continued rolling down their cheeks.

Now this was like somebody had dropped a bombshell.

"What does that mean?" Megha grew serious while I signalled the nurses to keep quiet and looked back at Megha with fake confidence.

"I will come back to you, Megha."

And then looked at the nurses...

"This is what the doctor has advised." I submitted.

"Has Sir advised intubation?" both asked the same question together.

"Yes, he did."

They stared at each other for a second.

With full flood of tears now rolling down their eyes, they departed, saying,

"If he has advised this, then it is okay."

Now was the time to face Megha!

"Tell me in detail what has happened?"

"It is the same thing I told you earlier; they will intubate you..."

"Then why were they crying?"

"Because the chances are remote."

To my surprise, Megha smiled.

"You took a lot of time to admit that." she placed her head on the pillow behind her and took a deep breath.

Not even a single sign of worry was visible on her face. Instead, she grew calmer, and that was what disturbed me more.

"How long will it take to start and finish the intubation process?"

"15 minutes at max." the nurse had brought the consent form.

She stared at me for a while, trying to gauge the seriousness of the issue.

I stood firm; she stood firmer!

"Call the entire staff in ICU here. I want to talk to them."

I told the nurse, and they all came around her bed immediately.

"I wanted to appreciate the way all of you have been working all day and night risking your own life amidst Covid patients." she started.

"I just wanted to say a BIG Thank You to all of you." she concluded, with a usual smile.

I could see the nursing staff shivering while she, on the death bed, spoke firmly.

She was required to speak with double force for her voice to be audible outside as her mouth was covered with the oxygen mask.

As the nursing staff started to leave, Megha noticed something in a male staff's shirt pocket.

"Which brand is this pen of?"

He looked at his shirt pocket where he had tucked this beautiful pen.

"It is a very costly one."

"Once I am back, I will give you one."

Another nurse came running as she learned Megha was going to get intubated. I did not want any more hue and cry around Megha, which might upset her mood or cause her anxiety or fear. As I saw her approaching us, I signalled her to stop on the way and not disturb Megha.

"But she is hungry!" she said from a distance.

Did she have any means of letting Megha have her meals? Can intubation be avoided? What does she have?

I immediately asked her to come to us.

"Didi is hungry. She will require strength during her period on the ventilator."

She was concerned about Megha being hungry. There was no alternative to intubation.

"But she is not able to eat as the oxygen levels drop."

The nurse immediately turned towards Megha and asked,

"Didi, be ready; here we have some kishmish which Bhaiya brought. Just keep your mouth open while pulling the mask up."

And she put the *kishmish* in her mouth in a flash, ensuring it does not take more than a millisecond.

"Sir."

I looked back at the nurse while sitting beside Megha on her ICU bed.

"You can talk to her for 15 minutes before we...."

15 minutes?

It had just been seven years since our marriage...

15 minutes?

Our life had just begun...

15 minutes?

I had just brought her to Indore...

15 minutes?

It was just three weeks back we were playing together...

15 minutes?

The Alphonsos were waiting....

15 minutes?

The dishwasher was waiting...

15 minutes?

Aarohi was waiting...

15 minutes?

All of us were waiting...

And here I had just 15 minutes?

They had drawn the curtains around us, covering her bed from three sides. I looked at Megha, and Megha looked at me. She smiled, and I smiled. She started laughing and I started laughing, and we laughed non-stop for those 15 minutes. Not even a single word got exchanged between us. They say laughter is the best medicine; perhaps, we were trying that as a last resort.

As time got over, I held her hand in mine in assurance,

"Do not give up. Just keep holding on."

"I know."

"Even if you give up, just bear in mind, whatever the scenario be, I won't let you die."

"Look back." I would look back to find her standing at the door as I would leave for the office every morning.

This was her everyday ritual. One night, I asked her why did she do so.

She was lying in my arms in the bedroom. We had recently got married at that time.

She did not respond.

"Tell me, why do you ask me to look back."

"They say, when you look back while leaving, you tend to have eye contact, and eyes speak more than words. The psychology is simple, when you look back while leaving, you get more emotionally attached. Leaving against will become more difficult. You stay there forever."

I got up from her bed with a heavy heart, not knowing if we would ever meet again. She still did not have a single line of worry on her face.

This book could have been one of the biggest heroic returns of the protagonist from the jaws of death. But God had his own plans. As I was exiting the ICU, her words flashed back in my mind...

"Look back."

And I turned back to see her once again.

The nurses had already drawn the curtains.

"Choice is yours; in both the cases, she has only 1% chance of survival."

Megha tested Covid negative immediately before she was intubated.

I had chosen a yet more difficult way for her to die!

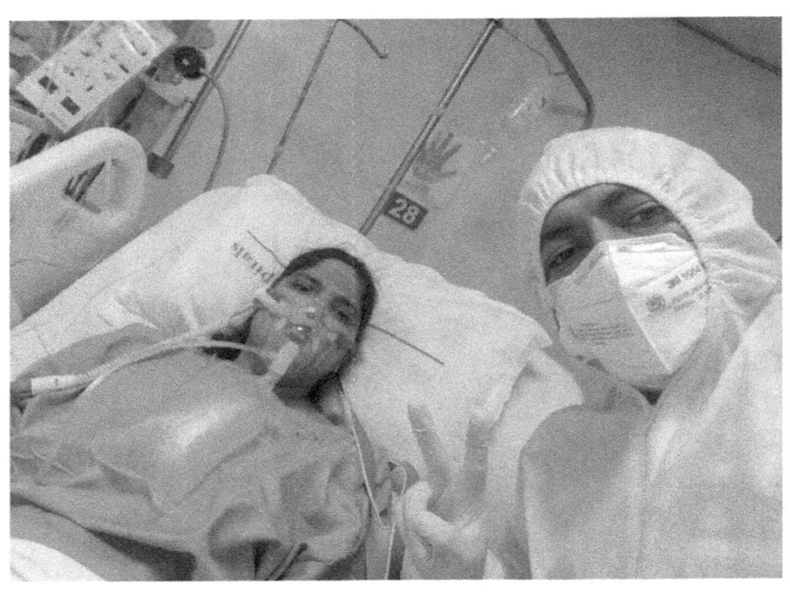

Megha on a video call with all family members immediately before intubation.

Date: 07th June 2021

Place: ICU Bed No. 28

SpO2: 95

Have you ever seen lightning struck by lightning?

Because there she lay, her mouth partly open with one set of tubes running down her mouth to her throat, another set of pipes running down through her nose to the food pipe, yet another set of pipes hanging out from her right-side lower abdomen for excretion. She laid still—the girl known to light up even the saddest of the

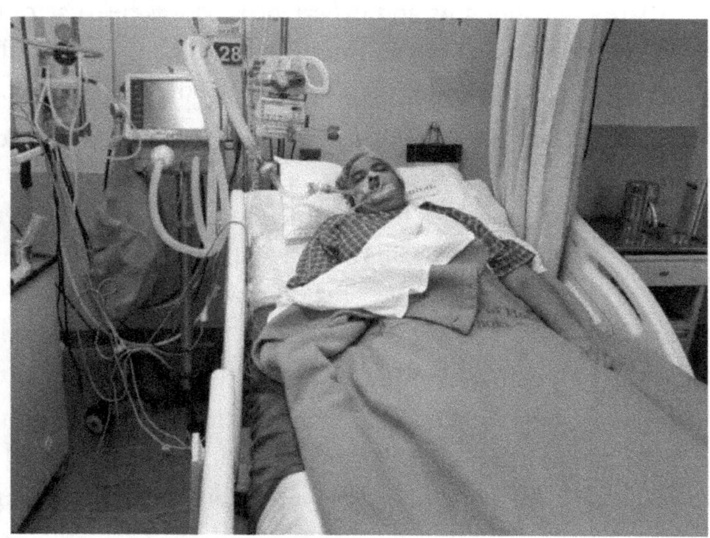

atmosphere—with eyes closed.

Her friends at office had planned an evening get-together at residence of one of them. I don't remember who, but some one of them was going to get married soon, so this was going to be sort of a bachelor's party. Both of us were invited. We talked about each other at the office so often that her colleagues knew me and my colleagues knew her. Further, she was such a social girl that you meet her once and you will start meeting her often. Megha was such a friendly being that her vibrant personality used to light up every room she entered. She was the epitome of social grace, effortlessly weaving her way through social circles and leaving a lasting impact on everyone she encountered. Her magnetic charm and warm demeanour drew people towards her like a moth to a flame.

With an innate ability to connect with others, Megha possessed an unmatched friendliness that instantly put people at ease. She greeted everyone with a genuine smile and a sparkle in her eyes, making them feel valued and appreciated. Her contagious laughter and easy-going nature created an inviting atmosphere, encouraging others to open up and share their thoughts and experiences. It was because of this that people, known or unknown, would never hesitate to discuss their problems with her, and she would take pride in solving them out.

She had an uncanny ability to make people feel special, remembering their names, interests, and personal stories, which added a personal touch to her interactions. She always listened attentively, engaged in meaningful conversations, and effortlessly navigated a wide range of topics, making everyone feel heard and understood.

Not only did Megha excel in one-on-one conversations, but she also thrived in larger social settings. Whether it was at parties, networking events, or group gatherings, she effortlessly navigated the crowd, seamlessly introducing people to one another and creating a lively and inclusive atmosphere. Her energy was infectious, inspiring others to step out of their comfort zones and engage in social interactions.

Megha's social circle was as diverse as her interests. Her non-judgmental nature fostered an environment where everyone felt accepted and valued. Peers, juniors, seniors, and even the maids, felt comfortable with her. People gravitated towards Megha not only for her social skills but also for her genuine care and support. Megha was known to uplift others, offering words of encouragement and helping them discover their own strengths and passions.

However, such a friendly nature sometimes spooked trouble. At times, upon her insistence, I had to personally speak to some of her old colleagues who fell in one-sided love with her.

"Tell them you are my husband!" she would say smilingly while handing over the phone to me. We had recently got married then.

"Husband? But I always get a girlfriend-boyfriend sort of feeling with you!"

I know I might not sound that interactive and this might have become too long for you to read, so let us return to the bachelor's party!

"Where are you, Maga?"

Now don't think the editor of this book did not correct her name's spelling hereabove. This was how these South Indian friends of her would deliberately pronounce her name. Megha was a social butterfly whose warmth, charisma, and friendly nature created an atmosphere of inclusivity and joy, and she would never mind such pronunciation misadventures. Infact, she had her own reply for such conversations.

"My name is MEGA!" and she would deliberately not pronounce "H," which the South Indian community is very fond of adding to almost each and every name like SangeetHa, SavitHa, LatHa, SunitHa!

Coming back to the hospital bed from the bachelor's party, here lay my girl, in stark contrast to her typical vibrant and energetic self, her once dynamic presence reduced to a state of near lifelessness. Tubes and medical equipments surrounded the bed, signalling the gravity of Megha's situation. She was fighting this MEGA war of life and death all alone as I looked at her with helplessness. Despite the life-sustaining machines, the MEGA joules of energy that once radiated from Megha seemed diminished, leaving a profound sense of stillness in the ICU.

Her normally animated face appeared pale and devoid of the usual spark. The lines of exhaustion etched upon her features reveal the toll her condition had taken. Her body lay motionless, weighed down by fatigue and the strains of the illness that had befallen her.

Within the dimly lit ICU, the beeping monitors and the sound of rhythmic breathing filled the air. It was a constant reminder of the fragile state in which Megha was, her once dynamic spirit overshadowed by the adversity she faced. The very essence that defined her energetic persona now lay dormant, awaiting the return of vitality.

Yet, even in this state of diminished vitality, there was a glimmer of hope. The medical professionals attending Megha worked diligently, their expertise and care serving as a beacon of possibility. The love and support from them surrounded the bed, fostering resilience and fuelling the belief that Megha may soon reclaim her energetic spirit.

In this state of fragility, the ICU had become a space where hope and determination intermingled. It became a place where the resilience of the human spirit battled against the constraints of illness, awaiting the moment when the vibrant energy that defined Megha would once again burst forth, breathing life back into her being.

I had spent the whole night going through research reports on

Covid. I was particularly curious to know the sequence of events for patients who reached the full-fledged ventilator stage. And every research report I went through had one thing in common.

"There was only 1% chance of survival."

One of the most extensive research reports said that any SpO2 reading below 92 would further diminish the chances of survival, resulting in mortality.

The same research report had yet another finding that Megha had already complained of!

"The pain is emanating from the spine!"

While I do not have track of all reports I went through then, but what I remember is that this pain that emanated from the spine, at particularly this juncture of Covid infection, was actually not a pain. It was the final attempt by the body to fight the infection. Only when all other body organs have failed to resist the foreign body, the spinal cord takes everything in its stride, giving the last and the toughest fight to the infection. It is like the queen in the game of chess going all out to protect the king with all pawns, rooks, bishops, and knights already sacrificed.

The report further stated that the spinal cord is a reservoir of many minerals and fluids lost during this fight against the infection. Once lost, recovery of the spine is extremely difficult and time taking. I do not know how true this finding was. Still, I could relate everything with what Megha suffered just two days back, why the nurses looked at me in ignorance of the pain, why the Iodex was supposed to be just a placebo!

Was that all Megha was going through?

No, because the reports I went through had multiple findings and pain points.

"The ordeal is so taxing that many wish for death. The patients cry—'I just want to die because this is so excruciating.' That's what this virus

does."

"Being in the ICU for any reason also vastly increases a person's risk for delirium, a state of confusion that can result in agitation, fear, and anger. Medications used to sedate people or relieve pain are part of the reason for this risk, as are the constant monitoring and physical disturbances—and subsequent sleep disruption."

"Many patients told how isolating and lonely it is, and many get depressed. It is also incredibly scary to reach that point of illness with a disease that already has killed many people."

"One of the patients specifically told me before I put the breathing tube in, 'Let everyone know that this is real; my lungs are on fire. It's like bees are stinging me. I can't breathe. Please let them know to wear a mask... because I wouldn't wish this on my worst enemy."

"Despite the strict isolation for Covid-19 patients, we try to make sure patients don't die alone; for those who quickly nosedive, there often isn't time to bring in their family. Those people die surrounded by medical staff, receiving CPR or, if they do not resuscitate orders, with staff standing by."

"For those who fall towards death, family—in full PPE—are now typically allowed in (which wasn't usually the case at the beginning of the pandemic). At that point, we would proceed with comfort measures only. In this scenario, the dying person will be on heavy medication as the ventilator tube is removed. ***Even still, once it gets removed, people often gasp or cough as the body fights for air before dying."***

"Despite the palliative care and the possibility for the family to now be present for a person's actual death, doctors describe Covid-19 as a ***uniquely terrible way to die.*** *Covid is just so different. I don't think anything could be comparable. I don't wish it on my worst enemy."*

Anyways, I was told that I could no more visit ICU four times a day. The ICU visiting hours were only once a day between 4 to 5 in the evening. The nurses said she would not hear anything as I tried talking to her while she lay unconscious in bed.

Megha was left alone in her MEGA battle between life and death.

The Queen was fighting the battle all out, keeping the King safe never realising it is the Queen that makes a man, a King!

Date: 08th June 2021

Place: ICU Bed No. 28

SpO2: 90

"Do you know Sadhguru has a daughter?"

Megha asked this question while in the ICU bed just a few days back. I had taken Aarohi with me to see Megha. It was like life had returned in the ICU, which remained silent as a graveyard. Many nurses joined us during Aarohi's meeting with Megha, clicking pictures on their mobiles. Megha was extremely happy to see Aarohi after so many days.

"Do you know Sadhguru has a daughter?"

"Yes, I do."

That was her 18th day in the hospital and her 15th day in the ICU.

"Do you know Sadhguru had a wife?"

"Of course I do."

"Do you know she died?"

I looked at Megha in anguish and pain. It was becoming intolerable for both her and me. She was not able to bear the pain, and I was not able to see her in pain.

Every time I went to see her in the ICU, leaving Aarohi in the nurse's lap, my heart would start beating faster. Despite all measures, the SpO2 levels were falling day by day with no signs of improvement.

"Ab tum Sadhguru ban jana."

And I ran out of the ICU with tears all over.

Somewhere in Aug 2008...

City: *Noida*

Event: *HR Interview at Patni Computer Systems*

Lady HR: *"So, Mr. Ankur, what are your hobbies?"*

Me: *"Writing articles and poems."*

Lady HR: *"When do you write such articles and poems?"*

I paused for a microsecond, expecting she would ask what sort of articles and poems, but she had asked "when."

Post this microsecond pause during which my brain could comprehend she had asked when and not what, this came out of my mouth in the flow,

Me: *"Whenever I am sad and disturbed."*

I kicked myself hard from inside as I had already cleared the technical rounds. This was the final round before we could negotiate salary with the hiring manager. The recession was at its peak. Companies had cancelled all campus placements. And here was I, diminishing my chances of selection with my silly answers, that too, in the HR round.

Lady HR: *"And when did you write last?"*

It was again a "when" as against a "what"!

Me: *"Two years back."*

I kicked myself again for such an impromptu, ill-considered, hurried response. Anything done once in two years can't be a hobby.

The interview had gone on the wrong track.

Lady HR: *"So that means you have been happy for the past two years."*

It was now that I realised that she had caught me!

Megha and I had been together since the beginning of our college days and life had been fun. I had always felt blissful in Megha's presence. Her infectious laughter and warm smile brought in a profound sense of joy. The shared memories, the inside jokes, and the understanding we had, created a bond that brought us together.

Nevertheless, I had cleared the interview.

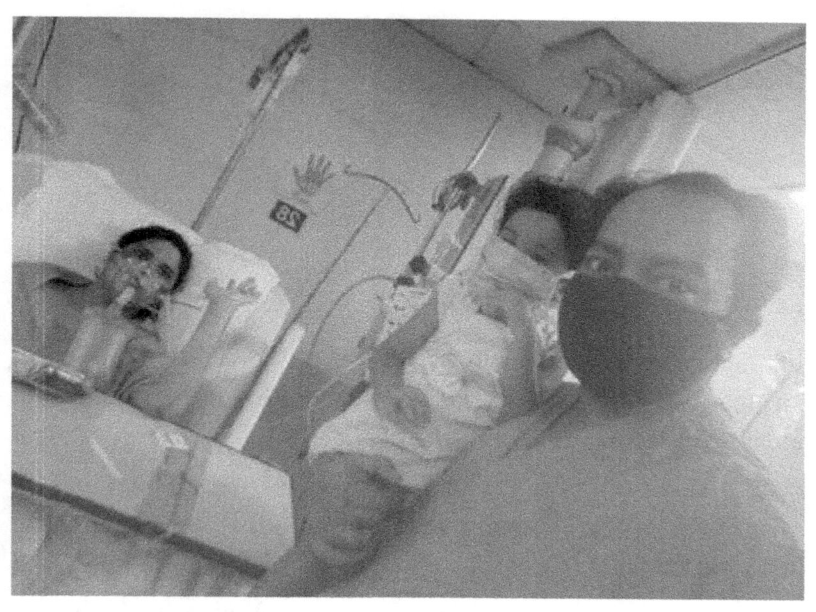

Aarohi's visit to ICU on 05th June 2021—one day before intubation

Date: 09th June 2021

Place: ICU Bed No. 28

SpO2: 91

"Why do bad things happen to good people?"

I thought, standing at the bed in the ICU while looking at her—lying on the bed with tubes going into her mouth partly open—unconscious. She was fighting the plight alone.

The increasing oxygen levels conveyed she was maintaining the requisite oxygen levels required for survival, as per research reports I had gone through.

But the scene, the way she lay there, caused pain. If there is anything called the ultimate suffering, it was this, where you see your love fighting against death, and you feel helpless, unable to do anything.

"Why do bad things happen to good people?"

Can there be a soul more divine than her? Can there be a soul purer than her? She was a perfect blend of tradition with modernity. You name any character or topic from Mythology and her pravachanas would start with a cent percent accuracy of facts and figures. I loved the way she celebrated every festival, particularly the Navratras, keeping all nine days fast, dragging me inside the temple in our home, making me chant all mantras. At the same time, she would read all chapters of Durga Ashtmi. A *teeka* at the middle of her forehead would add stars to her beauty. I was in love!

"Why do bad things happen to good people?"

"There is no good or bad, Ankur." her pravachanas started, *"it is all about perception, the way you look at things."*

I would continue smiling from inside without revealing this to her as I listened to her pravachanas, her lips fluttering against each other as she used to grow serious. At the same time, such discussions and such contrary cum temporary seriousness on her ever-smiling face added more glamour to it.

"Imagine me watching a movie and you coming late from the office."

"Achha." I said in a funny tone.

She punched me with her elbow in my stomach, seeking my seriousness in this serious discussion.

"So, imagine me watching a movie and you coming late from the office."

"Okay." This time I attempted to sound serious.

"Now, as you come in between the movie, you see the protagonist a very joyful, a very helpful person, playing with his kids and helping everyone he met. Suddenly, the police comes in and arrests him, putting him behind bars."

"But why would the police arrest him?" it was a deliberate attempt on my part to make fun again, but she was serious.

"Exactly, you do not know the plot, hence the question."

"Exactly, you do not know the plot, hence the question."

What was the plot here?

Each and every word of her struck me as I was asked to leave the ICU on completion of 15 minutes duration of meeting the patient.

I stood fixed there, trying to understand the plot.

It wasn't bad thing happening to good people; it was the worst happening to the best!

Date: 10th June 2021

Place: ICU Bed No. 28

SpO2: 88

"Bhaiya, give me ten bundles of bidi."

The shopkeeper looked at the guy who came down from a sedan asking for bidis as against cigarettes.

While handing over the bundles of bidi in my hands, he asked...

"Matchstick?"

I smiled at him and nodded in negative.

"Hello, Sir. The doctor has called you into his cabin. Please come asap." I got a call from the hospital.

I reached the doctor in a minute as I was sitting in the hospital itself, not having returned home after I came to the hospital in the morning despite knowing the visiting hours. I could not face anybody at home, her mom, Aarohi, and anybody I knew. I just wanted to run away.

"It has been four days that she has been on ventilator support. We cannot continue this anymore. We need a consent form from you." the nurse said as I tried reaching out to the doctor.

I broke down completely. What else did these guys need? I had already given them my everything. Why another consent form? I just wanted Megha back.

I must admit that we had got the best doctor to treat Megha. He was not just a doctor but a person with much compassion for human emotions. He held my hand and tried to console.

"What do they need yet another consent for?"

"Tracheostomy." he responded.

Tracheostomy is an operative procedure that creates a surgical airway in the cervical trachea. It is most often performed in patients who have had difficulty weaning off a ventilator, followed by those who have suffered trauma or a catastrophic neurologic insult. And this required yet another hole to be drilled into her neck below her vocal chords to place the tracheostomy tube inside, allowing the air to directly reach the lungs, bypassing the mouth, nose, and throat.

I had no choice but to sign the consent form.

I was supposed to open 2 bundles of *bidi* every evening for five consecutive days and put them in a newspaper, go to the hospital at her bed, swivel them over her head seven times, then reach an isolated place, throw the stuff away, and should not turn back to see it.

But while doing this on the third day, one of the nurses saw me in the ICU.

"Bhaiya..." I stopped.

She stopped me at the exit as I was about to leave. I thought she would prohibit me from doing such things in the ICU.

"I have a request."

It was the third day, and any denial of doing the same would mean that this—"supposed to be a 5-day affair" would stand broken, and that would threaten Megha's life. We had given up by now and yielded to the power of the almighty.

"Bhaiya..." she asked again, and before I could respond, she started crying as I turned back towards her.

I was confused.

"If you think you need to call any pandit or purohit in the ICU, I will get you permission from the hospital management."

I stood fixed.

"Just save her." And I melted as she said so.

I felt more helpless as these last three words came from her.

"I will." I moved on as I left her crying.

I told you, everyone she met even once would get attached to her for a lifetime.

"Only 1% chance of survival."

And I will bet my 100% on this 1% probability.

They asked to send this photo to her on her WhatsApp and ask her to pray before him, and we did.

They asked to paste this photo behind her on the ICU bed, and we did.

They asked to keep some *tulsi* leaves under her pillow, and we did.

They asked to place one *bhabhoot* on her forehead, and we did.

They asked to start *mahamrityunjaya mantra jaap* for her, and we did.

They said a yajna at the bank of Saryu would save her, and we got it done.

They advised, "नज़र उतारो उसकी *(rid of the evil eye that has been cast on her)*," and we did...

They asked to feed red-brownish dogs, and we did.

And they kept saying, and we kept doing.

Nothing worked!

Date: 11th June 2021

Place: ICU Bed No. 28

SpO2: 84

"Megha."

The doctor called her, speaking a little loud as she was under the effect of sedatives.

"Megha." he called again.

We all were standing by her bedside—me, the doctor, and the entire nursing staff. He was attempting to bring her to consciousness for a while. She was not responding.

"Meghaaaaaaaa!" I called this time in despair, and she opened her eyes.

I felt like hugging her, taking her in my fold, and running away from there.

"Everything is going well. Just keep holding." The doctor tried to communicate and boost her morale. She tried to nod and then closed her eyes.

"Alright, increase the dose of sedatives. You come with me." the doctor instructed the nursing staff and asked me to follow him.

He took the daily monitoring report kept on her bedside and

wrote,

"Poor prognosis on the ventilator with FiO2 100%, advised the relative of the patient about deteriorating health."

During the last five days on the ventilator, her platelet count had fallen badly, after which a blood transfusion was carried out.

Her haemoglobin levels had dropped much below normal, so another unit of blood was transfused.

While the urine culture had not revealed any infection, her blood pressure shot above 200, but she was fighting.

Nurses told me that despite the heavy dosage of sedatives, she kept gaining consciousness, as a result of which more sedatives were given to keep her *comfortably unconscious.*

A new cause of worry was some bacterial growth near the tracheostomy site on her throat, due to which PCT (procalcitonin test), which measures if the patient has sepsis from bacterial infection, had increased from 0.045 to 1.67. I had never ever seen decimals holding so much relevance in human life.

The virus could not kill her; the bacteria did!

Date: 12th June 2021

Place: ICU Bed No. 28

SpO2: 92

"Take Megha and Aarohi with you." I WhatsApp-ed her brother from my office.

It was late in March 2021. The cases had started rising. A second, more severe wave was predicted. There was no respite for people like me who were in this essential services category but were not vaccinated due to age restrictions.

If Megha and Aarohi stayed with me, they were more likely to get infected through me. This could have been avoided if both returned to Meerut with her brother and stayed inside, which required no physical movement outside. Megha was already working from home. She had stayed there for almost one full year after Aarohi's birth and had stayed safe. Indore was new to us, with no relatives or friends residing nearby. Though we had been away from each other for the past full year, one more duration of such separation could have provided her with a safe shelter.

"Hello, Sir." the lady said as I picked up the call. She was calling from my Regional Office. Before I could answer her Hello, she

proceeded.

"Sir, I just wanted to know when will you be joining office?"

The blood boiled inside my veins.

"My wife is on the ventilator." I tried to calm down.

"Okay, Sir, but you tested Covid negative on 29th May? It is 12th June today."

Any sphygmomanometer might have blasted if attached to me at this juncture.

"I said my wife is on the ventilator. I have a one-year-old daughter to look after."

She paused for a while. I thought she had got my point.

"But Sir Covid leave is for 15 days only, and you have been away from duties for the last...."

I disconnected the phone.

"Take Megha and Aarohi with you." I WhatsApp-ed her brother from my office.

"Okay." Her brother responded.

I sighed in relief. It may be just a month, and I will bring them back to Indore once the second wave ends.

"I will stay here with you only."

Her message popped up on my screen.

And I closed my eyes and sighed again...

Date: 13th June 2021

Place: ICU Bed No. 28

SpO2: 82

"I am sorry, Megha." I almost cried seeing her holding her head with both hands sitting on the divider on the Kolar Highway.

My leg was stuck in the bike's chain as we came falling on this busy highway from our newly bought Pulsar.

Coming back from the Antargange Caves on 25th Jan 2014, where we had gone with her IBM colleagues, an old fellow riding a moped in the middle of the highway abruptly turned right. We crashed into him while overtaking at a good speed. His manoeuvre was not expected as there was no cut on the highway. It was as if either he deliberately turned right or some force made him turn right, not knowing we were just behind him.

My helmet flew over my head as I had not tied it up at the chin. Megha tumbled multiple times on the road before her head hit the divider, and I got dragged with the bike with my right leg stuck under it. Fortunately, there was no vehicle behind us.

We had our marriage scheduled in Meerut just 3 weeks later!

Her colleagues came rushing to us. I screamed when they pulled my leg out of the bike's chain as the nails came off my right leg with blood oozing out. Megha sat on the divider holding her head with both hands, trying to understand what had happened.

I came rushing to Megha, seeing her in this situation...

"Hey, are you okay?"

She nodded in affirmative.

"I am sorry."

She smiled.

A passer-by put us in a car and dropped us at the nearby hospital while her colleagues followed us.

Fast forward to 15th Feb 2014, the groom had a broken leg while the bride had bruises all over.

We had finally got married!

Date: 14th June 2021

Place: ICU Bed No. 28

SpO2: 74

"Give me Death!"

Megha called from outside my room while laughing. It was probably 13th or 14th May 2021, when both of us were running Covid positive but were still staying in separate rooms.

"Go to Coimbatore this Shivratri; I will watch you on TV!" Megha said excitedly.

It was somewhere in Feb 2020. During Megha's maternity leave, Megha and Aarohi were at Aarohi's *Nani's* place. I was alone in Bangalore. It was not like she was your die-hard fan, Dear Sadhguru, but it was her nature to pick up everything good she saw anywhere, anytime. It was almost every morning; she would play one of your 2-3 minutes videos on YouTube after doing her morning Yoga and drag me into watching it with her.

"Good thoughts give you good vibes." she would say while hitting the play button on YouTube.

"While performing Yoga empties your mind, going through such good thoughts will fill it with good vibes and positivity."

I was doing just the second part just because she would drag me into it.

As usual, I always used to go by her advice not because she was the Big Boss of my house but because whatever she advised, the logic behind that was intriguing. Whatever I was missing in my life, she would fill the vacuum with her presence. Probably that is the reason why they call the spouse the better half.

I had booked my tickets to Coimbatore.

The arrangements were huge. Every person standing anywhere in Coimbatore appeared to be going to the Ashram. When I reached there, a Tsunami of people flooded the entire premises. I had and have not seen such a huge gathering in my life so far at any place.

And then I saw you, Dear Sadhguru, dancing and enjoying the beats while walking on the stage, going straight amidst the crowd.

"Om Namah Shivay" it came automatically from my inside as I watched the gigantic statue of Adiyogi in front of me, and then this book caught my attention...

Death.... by Sadhguru.

A bookworm had got his feed.

I had brought the death home!

"Ankur, look here." she pointed towards her feet. I followed her fingers, unable to see what she wanted to show.

"They have lost one of my bicchiya (toe ring)."

It was some time in the ICU when she was conscious, I do not remember the exact date, nor does this has any mention in our WhatsApp chats. But as she said so,

"They have lost one of my bicchiya (toe ring)."

...the page opened!

I have a photographic memory. It is probably because of this I am able to write this book. Even till date, I do not go to bed at night till I am almost half asleep. Because if I go to bed without sleepy eyes, the hospital scenes prop up as I try sleeping, closing my eyes. The photographic memory comes awake. The death starts dancing.

"They have lost one of my bicchiya (toe ring)."

The photographic memory started working, and the page of the book—Death—by Sadhguru—opened before my eyes.

"On that evening, a group of people from the Yoga Center had assembled in the shrine, as they did on full moon evenings. Vijji had already cooked for them. We were going to meditate together, and she was to serve them food after that. A few minutes after everyone had sat down for meditation and closed their eyes, she got up and went to the bathroom. I was a little irritated with this because once we sit down for meditation, no one moves even a limb, let alone get up and leave. But she went to the bathroom and returned a few minutes later. ***She had taken off her gold bangles, earrings, and toe rings, left them in the bathroom, and returned.*** *After some time, she just uttered 'Shambho' thrice and slumped to her left. And that was it. I noticed something was off and asked one of the brahmacharis to attend to her, and another fetched some water. But she was gone by then."*

(Excerpt from Death—An Inside Story - by Sadhguru)

I called the nurse immediately.

"Make sure her bichhiya on the other leg is not lost. She must keep wearing this."

She nodded in affirmation.

"No, listen; if required, put it in your record so that whosoever is on duty in subsequent shifts ensures this."

"Give me Death!" Megha called from outside my room while laughing. It was probably the 13th or 14th May 2021 when both of us were running Covid positive but were still staying in separate rooms.

"I am reading it for now." she entered my room as I opened the door and said no to her.

"You have already read it last year; why read again?"

She snatched the Death from my hands and left!

Date: 15th June 2021

Place: ICU Bed No. 28

SpO2: 9

"Once she passes 15th, all her kashts (sufferings) will end."

This was the day almost every *jyotishi*, every *pundit*, and every astrologer had told. While I have been agnostic to such fallacies, yet if there was something common in the verdicts or solutions given by all such men of supernatural capacities was this date—the 15th of June 2021. If she survived this date, she should have won the battle against death.

I reached the hospital at 6 in the morning to collect a coin placed under her pillow, which was supposed to be placed in a temple afterwards. The nurses were changing the bed sheets. Megha was lying unconscious.

I looked at the monitor to check her readings. It showed SpO2 as 9.

9?

I checked again; was it 9 or 99?

But the machine showed 9.

I called the nurse and enquired.

"Is there any issue with the machine?"

The nurse was silent.

"The doctor has been informed. He will come by 9."

The number 9 was now common almost everywhere!

Her Navratri fasts were going in vain.

All those rounds around the *navgrahas* in several temples we visited in Bangalore were all going in vain.

The doctor came at exactly 9 am.

"It is almost over, Ankur!"

"Almost? Is she still there?"

"Her brain is still working, and her organs are still functioning. Usually, the organs fail if the oxygen levels remain below 30-40 consistently, but she..."

"She is fighting." I completed his sentence.

The doctor patted my back and said, *"Call somebody from home."*

"Pack your bags!" I called her mom immediately.

"Pack Aarohi's bag too."

"What happened?" she inquired.

"I am sending two of my officers home. They will help you in packing the things. Then they will bring you to the hospital."

"Is Megha okay?"

"You can see Megha once, and then they will drop you at the airport. One of my staff will fly with you to Delhi and will drop both of you at home."

"But what has happened?"

"The SpO2 stands at 9. Megha is still ALIVE."

I disconnected the call.

Mom and Aarohi arrived in the ICU at around 1 pm. One can easily understand what would have ensued after that.

After around 90 seconds, I asked my staff to take them to the airport.

"Dead or alive, ***both*** *of us will reach Meerut the moment she gets discharged."*

I sat inside my car outside the hospital, it was 8 in the night. I would have preferred staying in the ICU with Megha but I wasn't given permission to stay there for more than 15 minutes.

"Once she passes 15th, all her kashts will end."

Why did such a soul warrant this much suffering? Her brain was working. She was thinking! What was going on in her mind? What might she have been thinking? Did she want me to stay there, and I couldn't? Did she want to remove those tubes that pierced her body, draining oxygen second by second, breath by breath? Did she want to say something? Can I be given yet another 15 minutes to talk to her?

"Once she passes 15th, all her kashts will end."

But why were *kashts* written at all?

Written?

She had asked me to bring her a notebook and a pen. I brought her Aarohi's notebook and a pen. Had she written something?

But where were her belongings?

The nursing staff had handed me over all the things—her mobile phone, the residual food items, the remaining homoeopathy medicines, the notebook, and the pen. But where had I kept them? I remember I kept them in the car's trunk.

I hurriedly got off the car, opened the trunk, and there it was...

I opened the notebook with teary eyes...

[illegible] [illegible] [illegible] [illegible] Best
chaha hai. [illegible] [illegible] [illegible]
[illegible] Prayka hai, God shd be with
me. Life Bhot achi chal Rahi thi, I
was very happy with Aarohi, I want
to live, laugh, love, God is great
Ankur Best hai. Solve the [illegible]

Date: 16th June 2021

Place: ICU Bed No. 28

SpO2: --------

So finally, we have come to the D-day. It is only now that I am realising I shouldn't have written this book, for she will have to die once again.

Anyways, right from the beginning of the book, it was known to both of us, you—the reader and I—the author that we were approaching this end. Only in hindsight can we see what was going to happen, and it could have been easily prevented. Still, when it was happening, no one had this much foresightedness.

The stars were against us, and so were the Gods!

Billions of light years away from this earth,

Somewhere in the lands of the Gods,

Overheard was a conversation.

Brahma: *I have already written death for three of them.*

Vishnu: *But they appear to be good souls. Won't death be an undeserved punishment?*

Indra: *Brahma, the creator, must have written it with a purpose.*

Who can defy his orders?

Narad: *But they are at Mahakaal's place. Death can't even touch them till Lord Shiva...*

Brahma: *Tell Shiva, I have written what I had to; I just need* ***three lives.***

"We will go for one more." he said.

We were having a casual conversation on family planning when her brother said that they would like to go for a second child. It was on some evening in March 2021 when they had come to visit us in Indore.

"What is your call on this, Didi?" her brother's wife asked.

Before Megha could answer, I interrupted.

"Sher ka baccha, ek hi achha!"

The discussion concluded.

I had got up early as usual and was reading some book in the study room. Aarohi and Megha were sleeping in the bedroom. It was the 09th of May 2021, exactly where we started this book from. I might have been reading for around an hour when I turned the chair back and found her standing at the door.

Now for those who have watched the movie *"The Wolf of Wall Street,"* the scene drew perfect similarity. Megha was standing with both hands against each side of the door, partly in sleep, partly awake. The body was, as stated earlier, glowing as Gold! You know which scene I am talking about.

"Who do you love more—me or the books?"

I smiled as she continued looking expressionless, half awake.

It was as if the girl was under the impression of alcohol.

"You know who I love more."

"If that's so, I want one more child."

The discussion, which I thought concluded, had again been brought on the table, sorry, on the bed!

"Tell me how many children your parents have?"

"Three."

"Tell me how many children my parents have?"

"Three."

"Then why do you want only two?"

She opened her eyes from sleep while standing in the same posture.

I got up from the chair and dragged her into the bed.

"I will give you twins."

Brahma: *Tell Shiva, I have written what I had to; I just need three lives.*

"Just three?" the Shiva had arrived.

"Just three." The Brahma answered.

"Tathastu."

Shiva smiled...

You can now remove your hand off your nose

if you have been holding your breath till now!

This was just to illustrate how she might have felt

during those 30 days!

I am sure you aren't dead, for you are still reading this book.

And I am further sure you couldn't dare do that!

But did you notice the cover page of this book?

It says,

"A Book for Just One Target Reader."

And if you think the book is written for you as you called her an easy death, you are wrong. Megha always said that forgiveness is characteristic of the strong, and I am strong enough. You will yourself come to know how it feels because Death has to ultimately come to all of us.

And if you think that the book is written for all of you whom she interacted with, then you are wrong again.

She has already touched your life.

I do not want you to be touched by her death.

But remember her words,

"Each one of us is capable,

do whatever small good you can!"

And if you think that the book has been written for you, Dear Sadhguru, because you found a special mention in this book, then no, you are wrong again.

Megha said, "*Ab tum Sadhguru ban jana.*"

Probably she was drawing a similarity between you and me based on the relationships we are left with—father of a single daughter.

But I do not find any similarity between the two of us.

While you might have gained wisdom sitting under a tree, I prefer standing as a tree against all tides till I get uprooted. I do not seek wisdom; I just seek Megha!

And if you think the book is meant for you—Dear Aarohi—for one day you will grow up and would ask how your Mom was—and since I do not know whether I will be there with you to tell you how she was—because life, as I said is a thin probability—you too are wrong!

If at any time you want to see her, just stare in the mirror rather reading this book, for you are a true copy of your Mom. Live life to the fullest, live in the present, enjoy every moment, always keep smiling, and always remember...

"Each one of us is capable,

do whatever small good you can!"

So, who was this book meant for?

Human memory is both temporary and finite. With the passage of each day, the memory keeps shrinking. An average human being tends to forget the incidents that happened to him a few days, a few weeks, a few months, a few years earlier.

This book has only one target reader, and that is the author himself.

For I do not want to permit my photographic memory to fade away with the passage of time. I will love to live the pain for my lifetime.

I just do not want even a single inch of Megha die inside me.

I know the power of my love!

“एक दिन मैं तुम्हें इतनी जोर से याद करूँगा

कि या तो तुम मेरे पास वापस आ जाओगी

या मैं तुम्हारे पास आ जाऊंगा |

पर मै मत समझना की मैने
give up kiya

Say Cheese...

Oops!

Say Trees!

www.ingramcontent.com/pod-product-compliance
Lightning Source LLC
LaVergne TN
LVHW012055160826
845678LV00014B/2836
* 9 7 8 9 3 9 0 8 8 2 8 7 8 *